THE TRUTH THAT GOES UNCLAIMED

Second book of

THE TRILOGY OF TRUTH

as revealed to

Jean K. Foster

This book is manufactured in the United States of America. Cover art by Bradley Dehner and distribution by The Talman Company.

The Talman Company, Inc.
150 Fifth Avenue
New York, N. Y. 10011

ISBN # 0-912949-08-2
LCCN : 87-050118

A
Uni★Sun
BOOK

THE HOLY SPIRIT

"The teamwork of this Brotherhood with you, the reader, opens you to the great good of the God of the Universe. Those who open the teamwork in this way bring you the gifts of the Holy Spirit—the undeniable access to what is God.

"Those who have wondered what the Holy Spirit means to them individually can now rest in the assurance that this Spirit is the nature of all that is perfect, whole, tender, gentle, powerful, creative. This Spirit is your contact to God Himself, to His great mind that pours truth out to you, to His great understanding which holds your being as His cherished entity, to His very core which proclaims you the inheritor of His gifts."

From the Brotherhood of God

THE TRILOGY of TRUTH

as revealed through
Jean K. Foster

Book 1
The God-Mind Connection
Spring, 1987

"The God-Mind Connection," which is the first book in the trilogy, opens the mind of the reader to his potential and introduces the Brotherhood of God. This group of advanced spirits from the next plane of life stand ready upon request to serve as counselor, comforter and holy spirit (communicator). The Brotherhood will help any individual build an open channel straight to God-mind, the Source of Pure Truth.

Book 2
The Truth that Goes Unclaimed
Fall, 1987

The second book in the trilogy, "The Truth that Goes Unclaimed," stirs the mind of the reader into understanding and being part of the teamwork of the God of the Universe. With the help of the Brotherhood of God, people may claim the truth that will make their hopes and goals realities. In this way each person is motivated into becoming one with the truth God has to give him.

Book 3
Eternal Gold
Spring, 1988

"Eternal Gold," the third book of the trilogy, has as its theme teaming up with what the spirit self knows is God-mind truth and putting it to work in the marketplace of life. "Eternal Gold" opens the reader to thoughts which will provide greater concepts of the God of the Universe, to tenderness, to prosperity, to wholeness, to energy that never runs out, and to talent that develops to the utmost.

THE TRUTH THAT GOES UNCLAIMED
As revealed to Jean K. Foster

testimonies about the Brotherhood and becoming one in spirit with God-mind truth.

Explanations of spiritual growth are presented which will keep us from wasting our lifetimes on earth. Receiving truth is not enough, according to the Brotherhood. We must become one with it.

Three universal truths are presented: one, a caring God; two, how to find spiritually compatible friends; three, how to find a true mate.

The key to enthusiasm is understanding the difference between universal and personal truth. Advice is given on how to handle depression, fears and disappointment over unfulfilled goals.

Explanations are given about the three terms, how they work within the soul and how we can use them to attract people who can help us achieve our life's goals.

Jesus, the Brother of Brothers, explains how we can demonstrate truth in the outer or physical world. Healing ourselves is discussed along with the wholeness concept.

An explanation of the earth's change to another polarity position is given along with reasons for the change, what will actually happen, and why we need not fear this event.

The metaphor of the wine and the wineskins is explained

with new meaning. The Bible and other truth sources are evaluated.

FOREWORD

Without going into detail concerning content, I thought the readers of this book might be interested in a few observations about my wife's free-flowing channel of communication with the Brotherhood. She calls them spirit/counselors from another plane.

Following publication of her first book, "The God-Mind Connection," in which she honored me by asking me to write the foreword, Jean appointed me as her official editor. In my mind, this has given me a bit more responsibility than simply to prepare a foreword to "The Truth that Goes Unclaimed," or to make certain that all the words are spelled correctly.

I view my job as two-fold. Obviously, my primary role is to make certain that her writing is easily understood—and grammatically correct. However, I have a secondary motive for wanting to help her in her writing and that is to give support to her belief that she is communicating with spirits from another world, that she is receiving specific instructions from the Brotherhood to write a series of books, and that the books are for the purpose of showing people how to gain the power of God in their earth lives.

We live in a university town where there are lots of intellectually superior individuals. Some of them readily accept the possibility of communicating with spirits; some are openly skeptical, while others are simply fascinated with the whole idea but don't really know what to do about it.

Here are just a few of my "experiences" of living with a writer of channeled books:

- It seemed to me after reading "The God-Mind Connection," that this book said just about everything there was to say on the subject. Jean kept saying that she was to write a trilogy, so I asked her what the second book was all about. At the time, all she had was a title, "The Truth that Goes Unclaimed." About 30 minutes later she handed me a 20-chapter outline for this book. It is the same outline that appears in the Table of Contents.

• When I queried her on what each chapter was about, she said she didn't know yet. But as the days went by, she produced chapter after chapter. I watched her as she wrote an entire chapter in one afternoon. Now, I consider myself a good writer, but there is no way I could produce that much material in that length of time out of my own head.

• These books are not my wife's first efforts at writing. While her earlier efforts were commendable, she used to struggle for hours over just a few pages of copy. The book material she receives through her God-mind channel comes rapidly, is well organized and requires little editing. What is even more amazing to me, the book is printed in exactly the same sequence in which she received the material.

• Jean sometimes receives material which is either disturbing to her or which she doesn't fully understand. So she contacts the Brotherhood for an explanation. Responses to her questions are immediate and complete.

• On more than one occasion I have run across some of her copy that I just did not understand. I would ask her to state it differently, and perhaps I would get the point. At first, when I did not receive an immediate response from her, I got impatient. She told me to be quiet, she was checking her "source" for the answer.

• When we go to church, she receives personal enlightenment from the Brotherhood concerning the minister's sermons. I hasten to add that generally they are most complimentary, but they do not always agree on various points of the sermon.

I long ago accepted the fact that her writing came to her through an open channel, sometimes from the Brotherhood, and more recently, directly from God-mind. After "editing" and studying her latest book, "The Truth that Goes Unclaimed," I am absolutely convinced that her material is coming directly from her God-mind connection.

Carl B. Foster

CHAPTER 1

TRUTH UNLIMITED

How can I have the power of God in my life?

"No one will ever be the same after taking these truths to mind and to heart. Therefore, do not read further unless you intend to team up with the God of the Universe, the God who will change your life irrevocably. Either read this book with the intention of performing new miracles, or put the book down now."

These astonishing words appeared on my typewriter paper one May morning when the air hung heavy with impending rain. I was receiving material for a book about truth, a book that comes through me, but not from me. The source of this wonderful truth is God-mind, I'm told, and I make this connection into God-mind through the Brotherhood of God. This Brotherhood is a group of advanced spirits in the next plane of life who are commissioned by God to be the Counselor, Comforter, and Holy Spirit that Jesus of Nazareth promised his followers before he ascended into heaven.

Though many of you may think it strange that I "received" the material for this book from a source called "God-mind," I assure you that what I have done is neither strange nor unique. The Brotherhood assures me that anyone, with a little practice, can do what I have done. There is no way I can prove to you that what I say is true. However, I am an honest person, and I hereby make you an honest challenge. Read this book. Your spirit will respond to what you read. Your soul will cry out in recognition of this truth, its power and the irresistible invitation to prove these truths for yourself.

And how do you go about proving these truths for yourself? First, you must determine your goals. They reflect the truth you now believe, and therefore, they must not be ignored. The Brotherhood/Counselor explains the procedure better. "Get in touch with that part of you that is your true self as you understand yourself. Then state those goals you hold most dear. No goal is too trivial, too private, too physical or material. These goals are your own business here, no one else's. Therefore, write them down only for you. Then we will go on with this book of truth to enable you to enter these goals into the encouraging forces which will help you create the life you want to live."

I set my own goals in the manner outlined above. Though most of these first goals are too personal to share, I will share one that seemed most important to me at the time. I wrote, "I want more energy." I lived life at such a low energy level, that just making it through the day became all I could manage. The Brotherhood commended my goal setting, and they brought forth the God-truth my spirit needed. I did the necessary first step, and they followed through according to their promise.

The second step in proving these truths is binding them into your soul as they are revealed to you. In this book the Brotherhood reveals a practical and ingenious method to do this. I can attest to the fact that the method works, for as my truth became one with me, I found a new purpose in my life, a purpose I did not ask for nor expect. And with that purpose came a steady flow of energy. My first goal, as you can easily see, had the cart before the horse. I asked for the effects of a life of spiritual purpose without seeing that first, I needed the purpose.

When I began my experiment with automatic writing, I received messages from earth-bound spirits who felt they must make contact with those they loved in the earth plane. But I didn't make this experiment to take messages from spirits on the next plane of life. I wanted a teacher, a counselor who could help me with *my* life. I asked for such a person, and then I met the Brotherhood of God. Advanced souls whose work is inspired by the one they call the Brother of Brothers, Jesus, began to counsel me on all the questions and problems I had about my life. Never did they make me feel guilty. Never did they expect me simply "to shape up" or "snap out of it." They are what they say they are—Counselors from the next plane of life who can help us achieve our full potential.

Becoming one with the truth of God-mind requires teamwork. "We bring the truth to the individual, who brings an open mind and an open heart." In writing down your goals, you have taken the first step in proving these truths for yourself and being part of the teamwork that will make you one with the God of the Universe.

"There is no way to be the person you want to be unless you take this truth we offer you now," continued the Brotherhood. "Only by teaming up with us can you rid yourself of the mediocre thoughts and feelings that come to you through earth-mind truth." (Collective beliefs of mankind, true, untrue, and partly true are called earth-mind truth by the Brotherhood.) "Your desire for spiritual integrity, for spiritual fulfillment, will not be met unless you team up with us to absorb this truth into your own spirit.

"There is only one way to belong to this truth we speak of, and that is to take it into the empty places that are formed by the longings within you. These longings form the divinity that is you. These longings tell the mind what they need and want."

However, we often get our truth from earth-mind, the truth that seems satisfactory for the moment, that appears good, but which eventually disappoints us. "The earth-mind wets down the wonderful spirit that God calls out for. Though these inferior truths bring discouragement, they also tell you that you must have the higher truth, the best that there is.

"This higher truth from God-mind will take you to teachings never before encountered. Then your life will change for the better and you will become the powerful person that you want to be. People who have no understanding of God-truth within them hesitate to believe what tremendous good can come to them. Because they have not emptied themselves of doubt, they cannot take this truth at its apparent value. But this lesson we present will enable you, the reader, to be the one to remove the blindfold and take this truth into your mind and into your heart where it will blossom.

"Only greatness will happen here, and only goodness will transpire within you. God's wonderful blossom will give its bloom within you. In your inner temple the teacher, the truth, and the reader meet to work together. This temple will bring forth the gifts of your spiritual heritage. These truths that we bring to you come from the God of the Universe to you, his own spiritual children, the sons and daughters of the most high, the true sons of God.

"You are never too young or too old or too unworthy to accept these truths. But to accept them, you must grow into them, unfold into God's children. Take these truths; you, whoever you are, take them because they are your heritage. You would take an earthly inheritance, would you not? Then take this spiritual heritage. This teaching enters your being and frees you of emptiness, of teeming anguish that strikes you down. You will prove that the truth is real."

The Brotherhood/Counselor promises you that as you progress in becoming one with truth, you will no longer have doubts about who is giving it to you or where it comes from. Also, they assure you that you will become whatever you want to be if it is for your own spiritual good. They assert that you will learn to use this truth to answer your needs and fulfill your desires. You may also request the energy that God provides. Then you will be invincible because you and God will take the plan you made together before your birth and enact it. No one can stand against this team of God and you.

"Never before has this truth been written. This truth has been told, but not understood. We will try to contend with this language that enters this writer to express this greatest of all truths. This entity who writes, who translates, who brings you this message from the Brotherhood of God, tells it the best that this English language can give, but it still is inadequate to the task. Therefore, this Brotherhood takes the responsibility of giving examples, giving anecdotes and teaming up with God-mind to bring this material as accurately as possible.

"We will open your eyes to the practical use of this truth, and we will open your mind through our teaching to the entire picture of possibilities. In this way, we will be able to present truth unlimited, so to speak.

"Give your attention now to the truth of our best Brother/ Counselor—Jesus Christ. He will take this typewriter now to bring his own truth to you, the reader. This is our special present to you and to the writer too. This person of Jesus now takes the keys of this typewriter.

WORDS FROM JESUS

"This is the truth that empties mankind of its tears over heartaches. People take their tears to the earth-mind truth that (says that) life brings much unhappiness, much to grieve over. But the truth that I bring here will take the place of this unhappiness. This truth says that you, the reader, are the child of God—the son or daughter—just as I am that son.

"Today we will talk together as family—as brother to brother or brother to sister. Take me at my word here. This business of being the son of God is not just for me alone. I mean it for you and you and you, too. No one is left out, you see. No one will ever be forgotten no matter where he or she is in the growth of spirit.

"God encompasses us all in love, in tender care, in His tender mercies. There is no thought within God to neglect some or to give His good only to a few. The emptiness that some feel, the neglect that some experience, the heartache that some know, come about because there is a misunderstanding within them about God meaning what He says.

"This wonderful God, this Greatness, this Truth Principle, this Bright Light of Guidance, never changes. He is always the same. Take what He offers. Take what He has for you. Take what He brings to you.

"There is more. Know that God wants to be one with you. Know that no matter *what* you think you are, no matter *where* you think you are, no matter *when* in life you come to this truth, this God you think you know will welcome you. Therefore, turn to His light. Bring yourself to His truth. Know that God wants you now, wants you as you are, wants you wherever you are. This truth will take you to the basic understanding you need before you progress to the next truth.

"My life on earth was spent in a quest for God. I lived searching for truth, accepting it, becoming one with it. My life was to show others the way to God, to truth. Never did they need to make me God as they did.

"Those who condemned me brought me to the crucifixion, but those who wanted me to be all they hoped for, made me God. Both groups were on the wrong track, for neither had the right idea. But God used the crucifixion to bring His greatest truth to mankind—that God touches us with life though we seem dead. Take this great truth into your spirit entities so you will understand that God is what He says He is.

"No one need stand aside, stand at the judgment seat, stand in awe of the wonderful person of God the Father. This Father I spoke of in my earth life expressed the nature of God that people needed to understand both then and now.

"Many believed that I went to heaven and to God because I was God. This widely held idea is not truth at all. I went to 'heaven,' because I was able to manifest my entire body to the next plane. This accomplishment is one anyone can do, if it is the wish to do so.

"But the main point I want to impart is that God is there for you to unite with. This is my WAY, my TRUTH, my entire TEACHING. There is no truth that can take hold until this one firm truth is accepted within you—that you and God are one because God wants you and that there is this relationship between you that is eternal whether you recognize it or not. You and God are ONE. To recognize this fact, to make use of this understanding, we bring you this truth.

"Take, eat—that is, eat this knowledge by accepting it. This is my body—my whole purpose for living on earth. Which is broken—teamed up with the truth of God, my Father. For you, the spirit entities that God wants to reunite with as one in mind, in purpose, in creative goodness.

"There is no truth that is greater than this one I have given to you. Enter it into your minds, hold it in your hearts, give it to your bodies to express. Then you will be God's child who is now ready to make use of all the truth God has for you to claim.

"This is the one whom you call Jesus of Nazareth, the savior, the way-shower, the teacher, the rabbi. This is the one who became crucified to enlarge mankind's conception of what the truth of the spirit is. This is your very own brother, the one who embraces you now, the one who grasps your offered hand, the one who teams up with you and this Brotherhood to bring this new book on truth to you, this reader whom I speak to now. Take, eat; this is my body which is broken for you and for many. This is our communion; this is our transubstantiation, our teaching that together we will be the family of God. Team this truth with your very soul. Team this truth with your tremendous growth potential.

"This is the time when we must give ourselves to the common task of bringing truth to all. This opportunity will bring you the power you may need in the coming days. This earth will undergo a great change, a change that will bring it greater beauty in the long run, that will bring it more purity, but a change that will be hard for those who have no faith.

"But for you who take my truth to heart, we will meet this change together and will meet it with courage and with the ability to carry on with the living of life. Together we will work out the requirements for taking people into safe places where they will flourish again.

"This is my best gift to you now, this teaching that we all are one with God. Accept this truth that I bring you, and the other truths will be yours also. Turn away from this basic truth that we belong to this family of God, and the others will not be of any value to you."

———————————

The message from Jesus completed, another spirit in the Brotherhood of God took over the communication. "This time we will work to temple the truth that Jesus gave you with the inner being." ("Templing" means bringing together or combining.)

"This truth Jesus gave tells the temple of your being the truth about itself. There is no temple outside that is worth the inner temple. The outer temples take their own individual truths to expound, but the inner temple goes to God directly, though with our help. 'No one comes to God except by Jesus,' it is written in the Bible. This truth is one that is often misunderstood. This truth tends to push this temple of our own being aside, if we do not understand the words correctly.

"Jesus gave the truth he knows is true. This truth puts us in the same category as Jesus. However, it also means that we have Jesus' responsibilities. These responsibilities mean that we must become the spirit that God empowers us to be. In other words, we must become our potential. No one may shirk this responsibility. There is no such thing as accepting this truth just a tiny bit. It is all or it is nothing with this truth. Either take it into your being and act upon it, or else deny it and go your way. There is no compromise possible.

"No one who combines with this truth will go astray. Nor will those who accept this truth for themselves unite with negative entities, with negative thoughts, with negative ideas. Instead, you will receive power, for your ego will empty out to be replaced by the truth of God-mind.

"You will believe that no task is too hard, and no task worth doing is impossible. That is how powerful you will feel, and that is how powerful you will be. There is no way to deny this fact, for the denial is useless in the face of the evidence.

"Probably you have never actively gone into business with the God of the Universe. Or maybe you have. If not, you have a surprise in store for you. There will be no thought that will enter your mind that is wrong thinking. There will be no waste of the talent you have. There will be the waxing of your talents, your energy, an ever-growing tenderness toward others. There will be a new understanding of all things. This wonderful change will tear away your former life and make it new. But there will be a better life, a better person, for you will find growth in this experience. And growth will last through all eternity, unlike the physical body.

"Teaming up with the God of the Universe—the highest concept of God one can have—is the basic plan before you can go one step further. If you cannot give your mind to this idea, either enter your own secret temple—the place where your secret self exists—to work on this idea, or just put this book down. The rest of the book will mean nothing to you unless you can accept this most basic truth that Jesus has written.

"We must give this challenge to you before we give more truth. The entree to truth is this understanding that we, with Jesus, become one with God. That we stand in awe of or even worship Jesus is the unthinkable thought. That we should emulate Jesus and follow him as if he is our own pattern is also unthinkable. This principle is basic."

In this way, the Brotherhood of God closed the first chapter. They put the responsibility on us for furthering our greatest hopes for developing our potential in this lifetime experience.

CHAPTER 2

HELP FROM THE "LOVING ARM OF GOD"

Why do I need help to claim my truth?

The Brotherhood of God, this group of advanced spirits who stand ready to counsel, teach and lead us into the truth of God-mind, are inspired and helped in their work by Jesus Christ. "We are the more tangible proof of God," they told me. "We team up with you to be the friends that you can count on," they assured me. "Open your mind and open your heart to this Brotherhood who stands there at your temple door waiting to be called upon to lead you into the wonderful life you want."

If you have written your goals as the Brotherhood advised in Chapter 1, you have made the first step in claiming the truth that God has for you. As best you can, you have now accepted the truth that you and I are one with God. But there is much more to claiming this truth than just a mental acceptance. Most of us need help in becoming one with God truth. The Brotherhood explains what it is we are seeking in the way of results, and how we can claim this truth for our very own.

"This truth we now take you to will lead you into unknown pathways, into unknown territory. It will make you the tender touch of God in expression. You, the reader, with this truth enacted, will become your potential.

"How will this come about? This will come through the team of the Brotherhood of God, this Counselor promised by Jesus, to the reader who takes hold of this bold idea that God can be one with him or her. Then when the reader has taken this thought into his open mind, he will be ready to team up with us to enter into the rest of the truth.

"There is nothing that cannot be taken into the heart and mind of mankind if people will team up with this Brotherhood. We stand at the ready, and we enter your mind by invitation only. We temper your mind to receive this outstanding new truth. This Brotherhood is the arm that God uses to help people use His wonderful truth. This arm is that which Jesus called the Counselor, the Comforter, the Holy Spirit."

I asked the Brotherhood why we must get this truth through the Brotherhood. Why, I wondered, can't we go directly to God?

"Going directly to God is possible for the advanced spirit to do. That you may understand this, we urge that each person try going directly to God. Take your deepest longing and reach out with it to the God of the Universe, to God-mind where all truth will be opened to you to make your life one of the greatest. But when you find this does not happen, when you find you still feel empty, then take the help we offer."

Then I asked about Jesus' earth experience. "Did he," I asked, "go directly to God while he lived on earth?"

"This wonderful Brother," the answer began, "went to God directly when he was in his last incarnation, but first he came to us to get his life in tune with God's purpose. No earth life is easy. No earth life teams up with God's truth easily.

"Do not be disappointed that Jesus wanted our help. Be glad that he sought this help, for now you too understand that he overcame temptations in the same way you do. He became the son of God, which is the same as becoming one with God. Therefore, you now understand that you, too, can become one with God. This true picture of Jesus is that which opens our minds and opens our hearts.

"These pure truth centers within you team you up with the truth of God-mind (the Mind that holds the truth of God). Now is the time to give attention to these centers, for these are the places where the truth of God will flourish. This truth takes hold at your centers, at your governing places, and then makes its way to the outer, to expression in physical form. This expression may come as bodily healing. It may be demonstrated through the energy that pours through your being. Or it may be shown by teamwork that brings your goals into manifestation.

"Teaming up with the Brotherhood assures all who want the truth of God that they will be filled. There must be complete assurance that we are here and complete trust in this open channel (the method by which the Brotherhood opens God-mind to the individual mind). No one can be empty of God truth because the open channel, which this Brotherhood can and will form in each individual who asks, will bring all the truth that a person can use at one time. You will be as the wind that blows on the great plains. The touch of this wind gives everyone notice of a power, unseen but strong.

"When you team up with the Brotherhood, you receive the following: first, that which is true, that which is honest, that which is reliable truth for you personally; second, that which will empower you to be the tremendous spirit you long to be; third, that which tells you that this life is the great experience it is intended to be; fourth, the truth that will em power you to be the great energy, the great talent that you want to be; fifth, that which is the best of the truths—combining with the understanding that you are one with God.

"No one will be denied who opens himself to the God of the Universe and who comes to God through the Brotherhood to help those who want and need help. Help is as close as the touch of the hand to the other hand. Help comes as quickly as the thought that reaches out. Teaming up with us is only a matter of will. Now is the time to enter into this team, this Brotherhood, this wonderful assistance provided by God and helped along by the Brother of Brothers, Jesus the Christ.

"The Brotherhood now wants to take you to the best truth that we gave you—the one we mentioned to you to help you become one with God. This truth is not too great to understand, nor is it too great for you to use right now.

"Our team teaches you to be one with God by taking you, the individual, not the group, to the emptiness within you that longs to have worthwhile thoughts. This longing you feel, this bright being within you that peeks out to find the God of the inner self, this being enters into this truth easily. First, there is a need or longing. Then, there is the truth center that cries out for an open mind and an open heart to team up with the universal substance, universal power, universal thought. In that way the inner self is ready for the truth.

"Now that this is accomplished, this opening up and this recognition of the longing within you, the rest is your own truth working within you to connect with the God of the Universe. To become one with God, that is all you must do—recognize the inner being or truth center, tune in to that inner longing to be one with God, then ask the Brotherhood to help you make the connection with God-mind."

The Brotherhood never hesitates to answer questions. Therefore, when I asked them how we know when we connect with God-mind, they had a ready reply. "There is one sure way to know when you have connected to the God-mind and no longer depend on the earth-mind. The person will then be his own person, assured, tempered like fine steel that will not break under stress. No one will think we teach false truth when we team up with God. There will be the authority, just as Jesus had. Remember how the Bible tells that Jesus spoke with authority and not like the other scribes and teachers? This authority comes from God Himself, not from earth-mind that may bluster and shout.

"The authority we speak of takes each person into his life experience to be the one who endures the slings and arrows of condemnation when necessary, but who does not bow to them. They fall around him as the rain falls, but they do not penetrate any more than the rain does.

"This wonderful powerful authority that God gives teaches a person what is important in his life. It teaches him what to do with life, with those relationships he works so hard at, with that vocation which is so very important. The person will take on responsibility with joy, with vigor, with great power. There will be no thought that seems too outrageous if it is truth, nor no task that seems too hard if it is the truth. This spirit will take on the proportions that make him or her the tremendous spirit that we all want to be. This is how you will know when you become one with God.

"The truth we speak of here tells us that we have much power. The power we have tells us that we can put our hopes and goals on the line, so to speak. These hopes and goals that we hold in our minds will come to pass if we use the powerful truth that we bring to your attention here. However, this truth we give you will not be perfected within you unless the Brotherhood of God puts this wonderful truth into the open channel that is formed between you and God-mind. That is the secret that isn't really a secret at all. The Brotherhood has always stood ready to put this channel through, to give individuals help in making a connection with this wonderful God-mind.

"Take our best thought that we offer you now. Take us at our word, take Jesus at his word, take those messages that we will bring you here. No one can put through this connection to God-mind unless he puts his trust in this Counselor, this Brotherhood devoted to your good. Then this channel that we can build to God-mind from your mind, only with your willingness, will take you to heights that you have never known. This is truth we speak here. This is the way to put power into your life.

"The power we speak of is that which takes you to your heart's desire, to your dreams and ambitions, providing they open you to your highest good spiritually. There is no way to put our good into perspective when we live our life on earth. Many make a choice that empties their good into a river of despair. These same persons blame God for that choice. They give the responsibility to God and say, 'He wants to teach us something,' or worse yet, 'He wants to punish us.' But these persons fail to take the responsibility themselves. This is a common occurrence.

"There must be the perspective we spoke of, you see. You need the perspective to see the optimum good for your lifetime. There is no other way except through this Brotherhood who can lead you to this perspective. This way you can see beyond the immediate choice to the greater dream, the greater ambition. The Brotherhood will take you to this perspective quickly so that you will not waste time making wrong choices.

"No one who knows the Brotherhood will be surprised at this claim, but those who have never heard of us may think this claim is ridiculous. That they may be more convinced, we make this challenge: Take the goals you have written and think on them in all aspects until these goals are as clear to you as the palm of your own hand before you. Then temper these goals with the thought of the God that you know, the God who is all good, all powerful, open to your request. Put these detailed goals into the hands of this concept of God.

"Think of God holding these goals. Think of God templing (combining) these goals with your own talents, your own character. Think with such clarity that you know that God takes these goals and your very nature into His thought. Open your mind to this concept. Open your heart to God's tender concern for you.

"Now unwrap these goals again. Tender your thoughts toward them. Have they changed? Have they altered in appearance? Have any of them dimmed? Take them into your mind and look closely at them. There may be changes there. If so, the changes are those that come to you from God-mind. No one can know how to make choices that will always benefit him unless this perspective is sought and taken into consideration. No one who takes this idea to mind and who turns his goals over to God will fail to get the perspective needed to make the wisest decision."

I asked if this is the only way to get this perspective. "This is one way to get it, the way that most people may accept, and the way that is known to work well. The next way we tell of is to seek the help of the Brotherhood directly. This way you have a direct contact that will take you to the same end. The way of writing or speaking that we give you will be direct.

"Take the writing, for example, that this writer does here. Anyone can do this writing if there is the will to do so. The writing enters the paper by way of our thought entering into her thought. But not just our thought, you understand, the thought of God-mind that comes to her through an open channel that we help her to form. This method has certain advantages for those who want the more concrete evidence of our presence and for the presence of the truth of God-mind.

"There is a simple method here, but it does take time to develop. This writer did not just sit down and have a wonderful flow of truth enter her at the beginning. There was practice on her part and an adjustment on our part. Therefore, those of you who want to do this sort of communication may do so easily if you will spend a short time each day, coming at the same time each day, preferably. Then we will tell you how to work with us. This may suit you well.

"Take a time period, however long, but come for 30 minutes at a time if possible. Use paper and pencils at first. Then when we get to know one another, we may move to a typewriter keyboard. This is what you do: Take the sheet of paper before you. Put your mind into neutral. Take the thought of some favorite place you have been—some place that is calm and peaceful, free of distractions. Then concentrate on that place until you are there. Breathe deeply. Think how you breathe. To pray to God is all right, but pray only that you may have light. Think 'God;' think 'power;' think 'truth.' Now you are ready. Take up your pencil. Then what we do together is that which must be done person to person, not teacher to class as we are doing now. Those persons who want to communicate in this way will be on different wave lengths, and they will have different truth centers with different power levels.

"Writing like this will work for anyone who wishes to do it, not just this writer or some other writer. There is no need for a seance or a special person to take you to the next plane to communicate. You, the reader, are spirit. This spirit within you wants to communicate with the spirit of these advanced souls in this Brotherhood. That is all it takes—desire."

I reminded the Brotherhood that many people are afraid of any communication with spirits. Many ministers say that such communication is wrong.

"There is nothing to fear here. Take your thought to us, to the idea of light, guidance, teaching, and above all else, truth which is of God. Then you will go where you wish. There are many spirits in this plane, of course. These spirits may wish to speak with you. But you need not speak with them any more than you may wish to speak with people you pass on the street on your way to your destination. We, the Brotherhood of God, are the destination. These other spirits here are those you pass by to get here.

"Yes, there are many who speak with spirits on this plane while they are still on the earth plane. But this communication is not the same as the one between the Brotherhood and you. The temple of your being cries out for God, for the truth, and that is what you keep in mind, not just the passing casual conversation of other spirits.

"There may be conversing between those spirits who care for one another. That is up to you. But do not suppose that just because a person has shed the body that there suddenly is a complete wisdom that knows all things. It is just not so. There is much growing to do among the spirits. They pause here between incarnations (between lifetimes) to review their past lives, to decide what they want and need to provide them with growth.

"The Brotherhood is composed of advanced spirits who give their service to those still on earth. This is our good pleasure, our responsibility, our dedication. This work is our vocation. The other spirits here who empty their lifetimes to reconsideration and review do not get involved in our work at all. There are some of them who pause here because of their concern for those still on the earth plane. They could go on to a higher plane, but they do not because they must stay here to work with those they love. These spirits do much good here, take their energy, their great growth to help many people still on earth. They better their own growth even as they help those still on earth.

"Teaming up with us takes you to the source of all good—God. Here is the point. The truth that we speak of in this chapter, the truth that helps you make the right decisions throughout your lifetime, is the one that you need our help to get."

I inquired if the thought process of taking our goals and our hopes to the God we understand and know is the same as going to the Brotherhood for help.

"This thought process is the way to proceed when you cannot accept the idea of the Counselor in this plane of life. This process of thought is one that will work for many because it is valid. The truth center of us all is that God-self, that inner spirit that we identify as belonging to God. This wonderful inner being we are will team up with the God of our own understanding to accomplish this perspective. The only drawback is that if the person's concept of God is weak, the thought process will be weak. This thought process requires a strong concept, the teaming up with the God of the Universe, the highest concept of God possible."

"So," I began, "you are saying that we can go directly to God, but the power that can help us might not be there if our concept of God is weak. Why is this true? Why would our response from God depend on our view of God?"

"Weak concepts wet down the power from God," came the answer. "Thus what began as a strong God-idea dissolves into a weak impression of a God who is vague, who is not understood very well, and even projects a God who not only has the power to judge us, but who does judge us. These various inferior concepts affect responses because *the response is dependent on our expectation.* This is the law or principle of thought sent forth to bring back the thought manifested. When we believe strongly, the power works. A weak thought produces a weak response."

I wondered to myself how going to the Brotherhood overcomes this possible problem of going directly to God. Immediately the Brotherhood answered.

"The Brotherhood enters into your mind to connect you with God-mind. Never will you receive a weak response because we are here to strengthen this response. This is our business, our teamwork that forms this thought of God into the channel that brings forth the wonderful truth of God unaltered, unweakened."

To test my own understanding, I reviewed the concepts in my own words. Those who go directly to God take the image they have of God and place it at the source of truth. When they place their dreams, hopes and aspirations into the hands of this God of whom we conceive, they wait to see what develops. But what happens depends on their own conception of God. If they think they are being judged to find them worthy or unworthy, they weaken God. If they think God might be there, but aren't really sure, they further weaken Him. People determine the extent of the power of God in their lives, not God. "Is this right?" I asked.

"Yes, you are right. However, this truth is hard to accept, for people want to think of God as a great power who makes their dreams come true, but yet they laugh at themselves for this hope. They 'know' in their hearts that God doesn't give things away. They write the scenario, the script by which they communicate with God. Therefore, the response will reflect that script.

"The Brotherhood stands in this place with the concept of the God of the Universe—a God unlimited in any way. This truth that God is what He claims to be is our truth. Those who enter the Brotherhood take this vocation to their hearts and to their minds that they may strengthen the weak concepts that others have of God. By turning themselves inside out, so to speak, they form this channel—at your request only—that will take you to the truth that God has for you. Then the truth will overcome the weak images that the readers may have. They use our image, borrow it while they are building their own strong God-image."

"The entire point to this chapter, it seems to me," I stated rather hesitantly, "is that when we go directly to God for guidance and help, we are hampered by our weak concepts of Him. Therefore, you, the Brotherhood of God, stand ready to let us 'borrow' your strong concept to reach into God-mind for personal and absolute truth."

"Now you understand. This concept of God is the all-important thing to hold in mind. The first chapter has the premise that people must accept Jesus as their true brother, not the impossible example. Then in the second chapter we give the reader an explanation of the templing of truth with his inner being. However, if a person insists on going to God directly, that person must take his own concept of God which will provide the limits to the templing process."

At last—I finally understood. I shook my head in wonder at this truth the Brotherhood explained so well. Then I actually laughed.

"Now the truth merges into you," came an energetic message. "Now you finally do understand it yourself. This truth enters little by little. This is what you are learning."

CHAPTER 3

BUILDING THE INNER TEMPLE

What is the purpose of an inner temple, and why must I give it so much attention and time?

Before the writing on this chapter began, the Brotherhood counseled me to build an inner temple. I did so, and I did it quickly. These dedicated counselors had spoken to me many times about putting my dreams, hopes and ambitions on the altar of my inner temple. Therefore, I built an altar similar to those I see in churches. I made the altar a golden color, and I lighted it with an indirect pale blue light. That was all there was to my temple—an altar and a light.

Though the Brotherhood was complimentary about my private temple, they gently suggested that I do much more with it. "Tell the temple that you have created to become even more ornate. This one is so plain! There need not be this plainness here. Take, enjoy what is most lovely."

Imbedded within me was an idea that I must not ask for ornate beauty. I equated such beauty with extravagance, and I equated extravagance with lack of spirituality. Now here was the Brotherhood I had come to trust completely telling me to build a temple of infinite beauty! "Just for me?" I thought. "Why must it be so beautiful and expensive looking?" Somewhere even deeper within me rose the thought, "What will people say?" They'll say, "Who does this Jean Foster think she is, anyway?"

Disregarding my thoughts, the Brotherhood pressed further. "This temple will be yours to put into the deep recess of your mind. Take it there piece by piece as you think of something you might add to it. Take the thought of pure beauty to this temple. Think the item into place. Build it bit by bit so that you have built the temple by noting each detail. There it will be, this ornate temple within you, this place of beauty, this wonderfully created place within you. This temple will be so clear to you that you could build it in this earthly realm if you would. But you will not build it on earth. You will build it within you. This is the wonderful truth we give you here."

Finally they answered my uneasy thoughts about building a temple of such splendor. "No way will we lead you astray. This temple will be evidence to yourself of what the child of God, the entity who wants to be one with God, would build to house the great creative spirit that God makes. No one would expect you to house this creative spirit in a log cabin!"

There it was again, that unexpected touch of humor. Certainly the Brotherhood had my attention. To build an inner temple suitable for a child of God—that is the challenge they gave me. My mind leaped with possibilities. I enlarged it many times over, and I removed the altar and the pale blue light. The beauty I added, the arrangement, the lighting, all contributed to my feeling of comfort. Daily I enter this temple—sometimes more than once. Here I am spirit, resting but alert. Here the true me abides. This spirit self is not Jean Foster. It is the composite of many lifetimes, many lessons learned in those lifetimes.

"This is the place where we want the reader to build," the Brotherhood continued. "This temple within that we speak of so often is merely a word we speak until it becomes real within you, the reader. Take us into your temple, into this retreat from the world. There we will work together."

In my own exquisite inner temple, my spirit self meets with the Counselor/Brotherhood who come at my invitation. It is here I ask for the truth of God-mind, and it is here the Brotherhood helps me make that connection by means of the open channel they help to form. We, the Brotherhood and I plus the God of the Universe, become a team to take this wonderful individual truth into action in this lifetime experience of mine.

They add a warning to us all about sharing our lives too closely with people who might have no understanding of the work of this inner temple. "Wetting down the dreams you have takes very little effort. This process happens regularly, especially when we share these dreams with others in the earth plane. Instead of wetting down the dreams and goals by talking about them to other people, take these pure thoughts into the temple you will build within you. Take them to the ones you can share them with, to the Brotherhood who view as sacred thoughts whatever you wish for and whatever you most earnestly want.

"These hopes and expectations become realities in your life when you invite us to connect you to the power of God-mind, to the source of truth intended just for you. This special truth, remember, is not for just anyone. It is entered in God-mind as the plan for your life, the plan you pointed to before birth.

"This plan—this individual truth we speak of—enters the spirit self by means of the channel we form to God-mind. The spirit then takes this plan into his own growth pattern, or true pattern, that which guides him to become one with God. The way a life is lived depends on how this plan temples or combines with the growth pattern.

"Is this clear? Turning yourself into a wonderful God-like person in this life depends first, on your recognition of the plan, and second, on the way you use it in the growth pattern. The spirit self who recognizes the truth from God enters into the bright team of God who works through the Brotherhood into your soul. This means you do not work alone.

"Does all this sound too hard? Too complicated? That's why we are here, to make the process plainly understood step by step. When you once understand it, you will take off to perform these things on your own. These wonderful miracles, as they will seem, will happen because you understand the principle, the God principle, that makes it all work.

"There is no way, however, to perform miracles unless you

can grasp our message here. Therefore, we will begin at the same point together. Then, my friend, we must work with you individually if we will progress. The truth we give you to perform will help you understand what we say.

"This is the way it will be. Put the temple of your inner being into your mind. It will be that place where you can put yourself at any time for rest and for rebuilding your resources. This temple will be yours only. None other is invited unless you decide to invite the Brotherhood to enter there with you. If you wish it, this temple can be our meeting place.

"The thoughts you bring to your temple are the basis of our work together. Therefore, do not bring aches or pains nor energy that has gone sour because of anger or hate. Take these negative things together and throw them into the trash can outside the door. There they will be sucked away as by a vacuum to become transposed into worthwhile energy. Then, when you enter your temple, you come into it cleansed and ready to realize your potential.

"Team up with us now. Take your thought to this page, to this word we bring to you. Take your empty mind to our filling. Temple your mind with the truth we give to you. Then you will be ready to hear, ready to listen, ready to enter into God-mind.

"At this point the Brotherhood leads you into a meditation. If you feel you are ready to meditate, read on. Otherwise, read the preceding paragraph again to prepare your mind to concentrate."

MEDITATION

"Take this moment . . . take this energy that is extended to you now . . . take this pure love that washes over you. Now enter into silence. Team up with this silence that will enter your mind, spread throughout your body to quiet you, to purify that which is the true you. Silence, now. Team up with this silence. Team up. Team up with silence. Team up with this silence.

"There is none other than God who will take this silent person you now are. This God-mind that you want to connect with will be yours as you accept it. The Brotherhood takes its stand beside you to help you enter into this open channel we form to help you enter this place.

"Now . . . Now . . . Now. Now the open channel is working for you. It is there to help you, to enter into your needs, to temple with your own true self. This is the way we will work. This is the way we will be there with you in your inner temple.

"New truths enter your mind at this point. Do not resist them. Take this wonderful truth to your mind, your God-given mind of the soul. Here these truths will be stored while you work with them. There is no reason to bring them to the attention of others. They are safe there in your mind. They will be open to your inspection only, for this truth is just for you.

"Be the one to belong to your own truth, to enter this truth into your own growth pattern to make this lifetime what you wanted before you came to earth. This truth is given for you, and there is none other quite like it, you see.

"Take the team of Brothers into your confidence. Take us into your inner temple. This place, and it is a place created by your own thought, teaches us how to work with you. What you put into your temple teaches us much about you. For one thing, it shows us what you think of the team of you, God and the Brotherhood. It also shows us what you think of yourself. Then we know how to work with you.

"This reveals too much about you, you think? You do not want to reveal so much about yourself? Remember, when you leave earth life and come to this next plane of life, only thought will be expressed here. There will be no way to hide your inner thoughts, for all may take them as you give them.

"Therefore, the sooner you teach yourself that thought must be open and honest without subterfuge or deviousness, the better. Anyway, these thoughts that you now hide are not the ones you want to keep, are they? What real good do they do you? They take away most energy and put the truth on its head. That means they do not help you understand God-mind, for they open themselves only to earth-mind.

"Besides, the way to manifest what you want and need in life is to be open within your inner temple—open with yourself and open with the Brotherhood who leads you into oneness with God. The only way we can work together is in openness. Think honest thoughts, no matter what they are. They may not seem noble to you, but if we are to deal with this not-so-noble thought, we must have it expressed. Then we can deal with it.

"Take this thought and others into your inner temple when we meet, and lay it down before us. This way we can work through the doubts, the angers, the fears, the disappointments, the feelings of hostility or the tendency to want revenge. These thoughts will be the ones we work with first in order to empty you of what is old. They clog the passageway created for the truth that will not only set you free, but which will also help you manifest whatever you desire and need."

I reminded the Brotherhood of what they said earlier about putting our negative thoughts and feelings in the trash can outside the door to the inner temple. Had they changed position? It seemed they were saying we should bring these feelings inside.

"It is our aim that by teaming up with the Brotherhood, you will rid yourself of all negative feelings and negative thoughts. If you can deposit them in the trash can as we said earlier, so much the better. If you cannot do this, then bring them inside where we will deal with them together.

"This writer presented you her own good picture of her inner temple up to a point. She must stop without giving details because we told her that her temple is not to be shared with anyone else on earth. She builds her temple piece by piece as she considers it, and it reflects her own inner tone or character.

"Under the plan we gave to her and which we now give to you, each person is challenged to perform this seemingly simple act of building an inner temple. But the temple is not easy to build when you must put in each detail. This detail, however, is our way of taking the individual into the concept we present here—that to manifest our thoughts we must be able to see them. We can use this same substance that we used for the temple to build the thought we plan to manifest. *Then the manifestation will happen.*

"To manifest your thought, put it into your temple where you feel happy and where you will enjoy tempering the thought into earth-plane reality. This place is all-important, for you must be without guile, without endless doubts, without the thought of ridicule, and safe from the powerful enemy that begets hopelessness.

"No one can manifest who fears the thought of help from the Brotherhood. Therefore, put your temple into place and make it your retreat where you and we can work together on the wishes, the problems, the hopes, the goals and all those matters which concern you.

"Team up with this wonderful opportunity to give your life more meaning, more power to perform the good you wish to perform. Never look back once you begin, for you leave the old once and for all. Earth-mind falls away and God-mind prevails. Therefore, there is no point in looking back at that which was less than the best.

"Moreover, there is no point in holding onto those old truths simply because they once seemed to have good in them. Tell yourself they are gone now, and you are now aligned with new truth from God-mind, truth which will last you all your days on earth and take you into the next plane of life with wonderful enthusiasm. Be assured that what we say is true."

Step by step the Brotherhood brings us into the knowledge and understanding we need to work effectively at claiming the truth that has so long gone unclaimed. Little by little we assimilate the meaning behind the words, and then we are ready to step out with confidence in those who give this message from God-mind. The Brothers understand all too well that our spirit selves grow slowly in truth. Therefore, they must teach us by repetition—reviewing the truth already given—and they must teach us by emphasis. Then when they add one more idea or concept, we can more easily make it our own.

"The truth of God enters you when you come to us. The truth of earth enters you when you go your way alone seeking help only from other people. To become the powerful person who discerns the true from the untrue, turn your thoughts to the teamwork we do here. This teamwork will result in your bringing our concept of God into your own mind to connect with God-mind and to become one with Him.

"Believe. Team up with us to enact the powerful desires and needs that you want to see come about in your life on earth. Believe in the Brotherhood which is ordained to do this work, and whose leader is the one of whom you have heard, Jesus of Nazareth. Believe. This is our present urging.

"Take this new idea we have given you into your holy of holies, your inner temple. If that temple is still vague within you, build it into the reality that it can be. Take into it those things you consider beautiful and restful. This place within teaches you wonderful things that become a part your being. Keep building and furnishing your temple. Use beautiful, wonderful things to make your temple truly a special place. Remember, build it detail by detail with your thoughts until it is that with which you feel comfortable, that with which you feel combined.

"Now go to work. Take all these thoughts with you. Believe this work is necessary, and then do it. This way the work you do will enable you to reach the next level of thinking without your realizing it."

At this point in the reception, I believed that the chapter was complete. I took a lunch break, and when I returned, I put my worksheet into the typewriter to ask a question and record an answer. Instead of the answer I expected, I received four more typewritten pages. The first part was directed to me to prepare me for the important material to come. The second part, directed toward the reader, was an introduction of the one who gives the message. Here is that introduction.

"Team up your spirit with ours. Team up to begin this next phase of our work together. Team up now. Take this God of the Universe to your own center. You do not know Him, you cannot imagine Him, for He has no limitations. Nothing can hold this God of truth. Ready? Open your mind to the unlimited concept that God IS. Next turn your center to this God that is unseen, unknown, the true God who turns us all toward the light.

"Be into this picture we present here. Begin to surround the entity that you are with the quiet purity that you sense here.

This quiet purity is God who enters this temple where you are.

"The purity which is God enters you and tells you that we now are one with God of the Universe. Now we, you and this writer and the members of the Brotherhood, team up with the purity to be the open entities who look beyond the physical to that which is of the spirit. We enter the work of becoming this truth in expression, of being the entities who team up to make this truth yours. The Brotherhood enters into this work with great expectations, with great confidence.

"The purity that surrounds us, enters into us, takes us in hand, enables us to enter into communication with Jesus who is the Brother of Brothers. Become one with this picture. Join with God's own messenger who takes his power from this pure substance, this true God of the Universe. Team up with us to receive this wonderful truth that Jesus himself has to give.

"No one can take this message as being unlikely or fake because Jesus has the authority conferred upon him by God to preach the message he most wants to preach. Here is his powerful thought expressed now."

TEAM UP WITH THE BROTHERHOOD NOW
Sermon by Jesus, the Brother of Brothers

"This is our truth we express in this way to the people who will read this book. They will understand our preaching because they know of this work we do here. Take me at my word. This preaching I do here is that which God wants me to preach. This pontification that appears here is that which God wants me, His son, His truth envoy, to give to you, the reader.

"There is no purity that compares to that of God. This purity will take its place inside you when you turn over the ego you now have to the God you understand, whoever He may be. This beginning, the truth that takes you step by step, teams up with your spirit to lead you into the greater understanding.

"There will always be greater understanding when you take your spirit self into a communion with God as you know Him. Now that the God you know is present, tell Him that you want Him to take charge of your life. Then wait. God teams up His truth with you to bring you step by step up His ladder to the ultimate concept of God of the Universe and to truth that is ultimate and everlasting.

"But you must always begin *where you are with the concept you now understand.* That is why I say to you to give your teamwork to the God you now understand. Bring this thought to our place of worship, to your inner temple. There we will work out the teamwork so that you may progress up the ladder of truth in action, so you may demonstrate the truth in the earth life you live now.

"No one will enter the ultimate the first time this truth is tried. Take hope, for there will be a time when you will soar past the other rungs in the ladder, past those steps you now take one by one. Then you will be open to the wonderful ultimate God of the Universe, and that will make us true brothers, the true family of God.

"Give this truth your attention. Take it to your mind. Team up with it in your inner temple that you have made so beautifully. This truth will be that which will activate the spirit into great growth, into tremendous truth acceptance.

"Needs that you have in the physical enter into the plan of truth also. These private thoughts about your needs and your desires will be addressed in your inner temple in the same way they are addressed when two people speak of important matters anywhere. This truth center, this inner temple, becomes the place where we meet, the spirit which is you and the spirit which is me. The implementation of our truth that we build into this book will make clear the position of the truth combining with the spirit. Take these thoughts of yours and enter them in your temple. Then enter into your temple in spirit, inviting us to come, too.

"The Brotherhood/Counselor who works with this writer is indeed the Brotherhood that I work with and in. It teams up with the person who brings the spirit self into her temple and invites us in, too. But there is no way we can enter this holy of holies unless you invite us. Belonging to our group is easy. There need be only the desire, the willingness.

"Take this truth now. Take, eat. This is my body which is broken for you and for many. Take, drink. This is my blood that was shed for you and for many. This teamwork is that body. The truth in action is that blood. Now, pour this truth into yourself as you would drink the wine. That is how we become one, you and I. It is how we become one with God.

"Now there is a person among the readers who waits to decide. 'This truth that Jesus speaks turns me off,' he says. 'This truth is too entertaining, not the truth I read in the Bible. This truth Jesus speaks here must not be from the same source!'

"But there is proof that I am the same Jesus who is quoted in the Bible. There is this person among you who questions my identity. But I am who I am, I tell you. There is none other who can give this truth to you with the authority that I give it. Therefore, take time to consider this possibility.

"Team up with me; I am part of the Brotherhood of God. Team up with me now. Team up with the Brotherhood to find out for yourself if what I say is truth. Then you will know for yourself, for I will come to you, and there will be within you great energy, great certainty that what I speak here is absolutely true.

"Now, go to the inner temple that you are building. Take it to your mind to keep improving it. Then enter there and simply enjoy it all. Teach your own mind the truth that there is no more objection to entering into this Brotherhood, no objection that matters, anyway. The truth will be yours now. This is my own sermon, my own message of truth.

"There it is. There it waits for you to claim it—this truth that I am that Jesus who works in the Brotherhood and will team up with you to bring the wonderful truth of God into your mind. Team up with us now."

CHAPTER 4

TRUTH THAT PEOPLE WANT AND NEED

Why can't I get my truth from others? What is so special about individual truth?

"People want the truth that helps them to live their lives successfully, that rids them of their fears, their endless problems, and their hopelessness. The truth people need, coincidentally, is the same as the truth they want. They need the truth that gives them the assurance that God is there, that God is real, that God is much more than they ever understood or hoped for.

"This truth, so basic to good living and good soul growth, is the same truth. Therefore, we speak here of one and the same, the truth that people want and need. This chapter presents the way this truth opens your eyes, opens your hearts, teaches you what you need and want to know."

When I first asked for a teacher/counselor, I hoped for a learned spirit who would help me sort out my life. I wanted a wise spirit who understood what it is that God expects of me and what I should do to live up to that expectation. As a little bonus, I hoped this spirit teacher would show me how to use my talents. And if it wasn't too much to ask for, I considered asking for a general feeling of well-being. I didn't want to appear greedy. I just wanted a little help in the living of my life.

Imagine my surprise when the Brotherhood made the same extravagant promises to me that they made in the opening of this chapter! Though I loved reading them, I just couldn't quite believe them. I tried. God knows I wanted my life to improve.

I tried to follow the Brotherhood's suggestions, but nothing changed for me until I worked at becoming one with this truth. Then, so help me, my life did indeed become better, so much better that I find the change incredible.

Therefore, don't be surprised when the Brotherhood says, "It's time to go to work." They understand our spirit selves because they are spirit, too.

"Take us at our word, at our promise that we will never forsake you, nor will we lead you astray. We in the Brotherhood are incorruptible. Team up with us now in your mind, then in your heart. In other words, think that we are here, and then believe it. Take your emotions and throw them into this effort also. Take us to be your intimate friends, those who enter into your lifetime to help you be all that you want to be. No one will ever help you in the way we do, so believe, enter your feelings of confidence that we are here to promote your own heartfelt good.

"Never mind if you cannot conceive of the fellowship of the Brotherhood. Take us to your mind anyway. Open your eyes to this great possibility that the Counselor, the Comforter, this Holy Spirit that Jesus spoke of really does come together here to work within you. Then there will be a surge of power within you. You will know we are there for you.

"In the second chapter we brought you the truth of your need for the Brotherhood's help. This help is not offered because we seek power. Here there is no power over others anyway. We are committed to this vocation and want to be helpful so that *all* spirits will advance into their oneness with God faster than they do now.

"To enable you to receive the truth that you need and want, we must bring you our concept of God, this great, wonderful and unlimited concept that you may borrow to make your own connection with God-mind. Then you will grow spiritually to that advanced spirit who is one with God and who can make his own connection with God.

"The Brotherhood waits to help you, and we take our understanding and our truth to those who ask. There is a way we can help this reader to attain whatever is wanted if it is in the spiritual good. We speak the truth here, the truth which brings you assurance that God is real and that you will receive His touch of good.

"To become the person who takes his good from the Brotherhood, turn to the inner being which governs you. This inner being tells us, the spirit entities from the Brotherhood, that you want this help for your lifetime. Take us into your mind. Treat us as guests who come to be of help to you. Treat us as the team that you want to be part of. Turn to the Brotherhood to become the person you most want to become—one with the God of the Universe."

When I first saw this goal on my typewriter paper as you see it now, I wasn't sure I should reach for such a lofty relationship. Perhaps others will hesitate, as I did, at such a prospect. As usual, the Brotherhood has an answer for us.

"There is no way you can ever become more than what you are supposed to be. Take that negative thought to the trash barrel. You are supposed to be that marvelous God-self that takes your talent to the earth while there and to this plane when you come here. There is no limitation on you. Take this truth to your inner being and multiply the concept over and over until it becomes that which has your picture on it. Then you will believe that you unite with us to become the unlimited person you want to be, and you will accept it into your heart of hearts. This truth of the unlimited person who goes to the unlimited God is our best truth to you."

What a far cry this concept is from the one I had of myself when I first began my counseling sessions with the Brotherhood. To think of myself as an unlimited person is not easy. I began with my spirit self, as the Counselor suggested, and slowly I built a concept of unlimited freedom of expression. I am still working, of course, with taking this concept into the outer person, the body my spirit self inhabits. But putting this unlimited concept of myself into this lifetime experience is my present goal. Fortunately I have these fine, loyal and loving friends from the Brotherhood to assist me.

You can count on the Brotherhood, and when they say, "Take us into your confidence," unleash every thought. "Take us into your heart of hearts," they plead, and you need never fear betrayal. "Take us into your doubts, into your fears, into your thoughts that unseat the truth of this work. Take us to your closed places where you take no one else. Then we will bring the light of God with us and illuminate everything with God's light, with God's guidance, His love, His belief in you as a person who turns toward the light to become wonderful.

"Never behold us in the way that some behold eerie ghosts. There is nothing eerie here. There is nothing that is teaming up with weird things of the imagination. Nothing about us is abnormal. The spirit self is not abnormal. The spirit is the reality of us all. This reality is not seen by earth eyes, but that is because the earth eyes were not meant to behold the spirit.

"There is an ever-present challenge during each individual's lifetime. Those who do not see the spirit can be blessed anyway—if they accept this spirit as their reality. This pontification (writing and speaking about spiritual matters) we give here tells the truth, not a falsehood. Take away the blinders that you wear when speaking of the spirit. Take away the thought that there is nothing real except that which is visible. This is not so and you know it.

"Microscopes reveal the entire life within a drop of water. Telescopes reveal the planets and the stars. The naked eye reveals wonders if the person stops to admire them. But the spirit is that which is unseen by most—not all. There are some who see on the plane of earth as well as on the plane where we are. They think it most natural, but they are exceptions.

"This writer sees only on the earth plane. She joins with us so that we may help her meet her inability to see beyond her physical world. There is a point of blindness, but there is still more to life. The writer takes this point of blindness to reach out anyway into the thought that we are here, and lo, we are here for her.

"The Brotherhood speaks, but only a few listen. The truth that pours through us from God-mind is not heard by many, for they are deaf to us. The writer is deaf to us too, but she does not let this disability teach her that we do not exist. The disability is something merely to go beyond, to extend over, to grow over. The truth we give to you takes you to the next plane of life to view what is there, to find out what we can do to help you in your lifetime here on earth.

"The reality that we are unveils the truth that you need and want. But without this unveiling, there is nothing except hope, vague and unlikely. Tend to the truth we extend to you that the second plane of life is real, that the Brotherhood is real, that there is the possibility that you may unlock all the doors that you now keep closed and let in the light of God. There will be no more darkness once you team up with us here. This is our promise."

In our first book, "The God-Mind Connection," the Brotherhood devoted an entire chapter to the next plane of life, answering question after question that I put to them. They described a place where our spirit selves go to review our lives and to determine what more we need do to become one with God.

They explained that spirits cluster on the next plane according to their growth patterns, which correspond roughly to our belief patterns. The spirits cluster in much the same way that chemicals are drawn together to make compounds. Each cluster of spirits creates its own environment by means of thought. Some clusters create a world of beauty and goodness and joy. Others create a world of fear and guilt where they work continually to deserve God's goodness. In the next plane of life thought is the key to substance. We create what we think. However, the Brotherhood insists that even on the earth plane we can create what we think. And they will show each person how to accomplish this.

"This writer teaches you something here. She teams up with us though she neither sees nor hears us. Teamwork is the phenomenon which gives you power in your life to become that which the truth can make you—one with God, powerful in the way that God is powerful, rich in the way that God is rich, loved in the way that God loves—to the point of seeking no return.

"People cry out for love. By teaming up with us, you will bring love into your life, into your individual world. Be the person who will have his great reward in the here and now, not in an after-life. Turning yourself to this teamwork will bring your life the purpose and reward that everyone wants in his heart of hearts.

"The truth that will come to you is tailor made, not group made. There is only one way to take the truth we have to give, and that is as an individual on the basis of one to one. The truth we bring is not that which is for all. This truth is for you, for the living of your own life.

"There is no truth that comes to you in groups that will make you one with God. For example, let us look at truth we learn from churches. This truth may or may not be good for us. Church truth is given out indiscriminately, without regard for your own growth or your own needs or your own desires. Church truth is told over and over, and it belongs to the ministers who give it.

"Truth is emptied on you, but it may not speak to your own heart at all. That is why we tell you to turn to us to get the truth from God through the open channel that we will help form from you to God. This channel work is what we do best. Even the Brotherhood does not know what truth your own soul needs. Only your own soul knows this for sure. But we can help you get what you need. This is our promise to you."

To be very sure I understood the Brotherhood correctly, I asked if the truth that people want and need is *individual truth*. This is the answer. "They want truth that comes just for them, not for the crowd. The crowd truth is not satisfying. It is not in their personal interest.

"People who go to church try to apply crowd truth to themselves, and many go far in their spiritual development. They want to be the entities who take Jesus Christ into their hearts, whatever that means to them. But they take the truth they hear and read in the Bible to merge it all into what they see as the perfect spirituality. Then they try to measure themselves against this thought. But the comparison only serves to discourage many of them. They take this truth into their hearts, and if they find themselves wanting, they think they have failed God. Then comes the guilt, the continuous confession, the anger they feel but are afraid to show, the hopelessness in their quest for God.

"There is no way to become God's person when feelings of guilt persist. There is no way to become God's person when people think they fail Him. There is only one way to be rid of such erroneous thinking: team up with us to hear the truth that God has for you. Believe in God's goodness, His understanding, His love, His thought that you will be one with Him.

"There is no teaming up with the God you *fear,* is there? There is no uniting with the God who will *punish* you for not being perfect, now is there? These foolish concepts of God prevent your coming close to Him. The truth you seek becomes illusive when you stand afar and worship but think yourself unworthy of God's attention. The truth you want will not be denied you if you borrow us, as it were. Borrow our strong God concept, borrow our understanding, borrow our team to enter into the wonderful truth you seek."

I reminded the Brotherhood that they often use Christian churches as examples, but what about synagogues or mosques?

"These, too, take their truth from a book they hold in high regard," the Brotherhood answered. "They persist in teaching themselves the same things over and over even though God's truth may be new—that is, new to them. They close the door on new truth. They cling only to that which was given a long, long time ago in earth time. They refuse to let God enter new truth. In this way they limit God, they push Him into their own concepts and call their concepts the *absolute truth.* That way they cannot progress, they cannot grow."

I asked the Brotherhood if there was some example they might give that would explain how God-truth helps people to live successful lives and to grow spiritually.

"The truth you speak of differs from person to person, of

course. Therefore, the reader must understand that an example we give is not the pattern for him or her. The example is only that—an example.

"There was a person on earth who finally took himself to our Brotherhood to learn how to get true success. This person wanted to turn his life into a big success by earth standards. He gave his energy to his work, and he reached out every time to take the top job offered, no matter if he felt qualified or not.

"Then he began to suffer because he found self doubt. His thought went from success orientation to failure orientation. Therefore, he began to fail at his work. Then he came to us, to the Brotherhood, to our good news. He began to see the truth he needed to take—the success truth. But this truth led him into success in a way he never expected.

"For to tell the truth, and he did just that, he did not want to do this kind of work at all. He chose it because he wanted to be a success and make money. Those two reasons were not enough to last a lifetime. In fact, they led him away from the thought of successful living. Then when he took himself to the power of God-mind, he saw himself clearly. He withdrew from the work he did not like, and he went into work for which he was really suited. He worked with real truth inside him, with real energy, with true perspective.

"This person managed to use the talent he had to work well with other people, something he had never done before. This person worked with joy in his heart because he was in the right vocation, the one he took pleasure in. He allied himself with us that God's truth might pour through to him. Therefore, he entered the good life here on earth happy, prosperous, healthy, and full of the love that God expressed through him and to him.

"This person is what you would call a big success, but when he first took this truth to himself, he thought things were falling apart for him. He no longer wanted to work for that company, you see. He knew he must get out of there. He felt that his life was getting out of control for awhile. But he persisted in taking this truth and using it in his life. Then he found his true vocation, the one he might have found earlier if he had been tuned into God-mind truth."

I appreciated the anecdote so much that I asked for another.

"There was another entity, this one a woman, who took her truth from God-mind right from the beginning of her life on earth. This person turned her life over to the truth without impatience. She emptied her own ego to become a person who was filled by God-mind. Then she grew into the wonderful person she wanted to be right there on the earth plane.

"She had an open mind, you see, and an open heart. This woman went straight to her own truth from God. She did not take truth from other people. She took herself to this God-truth in spite of pressure of others to make her conform to their point of view. She wavered slightly from time to time, but she did not let go of her own concept. That is why she had such power. A person's own truth gives this power. Therefore, this woman took her power to her work, to her family, and she never hesitated about the rightness of her actions. This is the way life is when a person is tuned into God-mind."

What do you see from your perspective about those in the earth plane—how they live and how they can improve?

"Those persons who cry out for help but know not to whom they cry—they are the most touching. They moan, they cry, they plead. But they never go to the source of power. They just empty their grief into the atmosphere. Those people could take hold of their lives if they would empty themselves of self-pity long enough to ask us for help. They can take their agonies to us where we can help them overcome them. They can turn their handicaps to our help, to our healing. They can work through the Brotherhood to become whole in mind, whole in spirit, and even whole in body.

"Instead, they weep because they have not what others have; they weep because they find no hope for living, and they weep for reasons even they cannot explain. They give themselves over to weeping, not joining the team that will bring them hope, that will prevent agony from entering or lingering. Those who weep will be comforted by this Comforter if they turn to us.

"The weeping we speak of here takes itself to other situations too. Even our best people on earth weep from time to time. They sometimes weep into the darkness of their minds because they momentarily lose their way. They think thoughts of discouragement, revenge, joining with the speaking and thinking that gives no hope for mankind. They often regard themselves as the 'lucky ones' rather than the ones who team up with the Brotherhood. They believe they have 'luck' instead of 'truth.' Then they feel sorry to be the good truth in action when others have so little.

"But they get off the track when they do this, of course. To teach others the way to attain truth, that is the way, not to feel sorry for them or to enter into the society that feels superior to others, or to become those who think they must give things to others to bring them up to their manifestation level. Those who do not manifest what they need in life will not prosper because the power within them is dissipated. This power dissipates into the entity's expression of inferiority, into his insistence that others give to his needs. He takes no responsibility to manifest his needs himself. It is the teaching that needs to go out, not things.

"The person who prospers must not neglect the needs of others. However, he must understand that truth is what people need, not just things. Therefore, the prosperous person has the needy person's welfare at heart when he teaches that person not to depend on people, but on the source, the God of the Universe. The truth of God-mind is there for all, not just a few. Not that we should not give, but we must give what is earth and we must give what is spirit. It is our truth that entities in the earth plane are both flesh and spirit.

"There is much truth that goes unclaimed because people do not know how to claim it. They open their hearts to the need, but they do not get much value teaming up with just their needs. They also open their hearts to their life's goals, but they team up with the goals only, not the power that can make their goals real. They must take their needs and their goals into their God-selves, their inner beings, their best selves. Then those needs and goals will be refined by God who will work to bring them into manifestation, whatever they are.

"The God of the Universe who takes you to His heart on these matters will not deny you anything that you can clearly take into your inner self if it is for your spiritual good. The

God of the Universe would not give you anything to harm your growth in this lifetime. This stipulation is not an empty promise. It is given only to reinforce the goodness of God.

"God has a wonderful life in mind for you. He wants to keep your life on its growth pattern so that you may prosper. The truth is not to be toned down into empty hopes. The truth is not to dissolve into the thought that God will NOT give you what you want after all. He WILL give to you what you can clearly take into your inner being, your spirit self, this reality that endures forever. This place is the real you, the real person we speak to here. Your body is the temporary home you have here. But nevertheless, we understand that you think it very important, this body and this lifetime. Therefore, take the truth to your inner self that you may manifest the things and the conditions that you want in your lifetime here in this earth plane.

"There is more on this matter. Take no extra thought of what you will take to this inner self of yours. Take those things, those ideas that seem important at the time. These will be refined by God, as we said before. These things will be put into perspective.

"Then you will take them out into the sun, the great illumination that God gives. They will manifest with the clarity with which you clothe the thing or the idea. Team up with us to accomplish this in your life. Take this thought often to your inner self. It need not be the one time thing, you know. This wonderful procedure is to be used often, not just sometimes. The more you use it, the better it will work, for you will see the true picture, not a vague one.

"Take the teamwork we give you now. This great concept of God is ours. Team up with us that you may use it, too. Team up with us to improve your own concept, your own faith in God's goodness. Team up with us to become the wonderful person you want to become."

CHAPTER 5

HOW TO ATTAIN YOUR HEART'S DESIRE

How can I overcome my fears, my uncertainties and my doubts about God?

"Open your eyes to everything you may take into your soul to make your dreams come true. Enter into a confident partnership with the Brotherhood of God in order to know your potential. We wait only to be called to help you, to encourage you, to give you the truth channel to God-mind. This is our pledge to you—to unite with you when you invite us, to bring the best that we have in the way of truth, to give you the chance to be the person you want to be in this lifetime."

My spirit/counselor from the Brotherhood thus began Chapter 5. The words of this chapter came to me in a great torrent of excitement, pouring through my mind and fingers so fast that it took deep concentration to get it all down.

"There is entirely too much focus on the God whom some blame for their misfortunes," the Brotherhood stated. "They say they pray amiss, perhaps. Then they say God empties His wrath upon them, or God takes their good away in order to teach them great lessons. This invented God does not exist at all. He is merely a great misconception.

"Team up with the Brotherhood to learn a new way of thinking. God is the One you hope for when you call Him Father, the

One who loves us all. This God, the One we speak of now, gives us power to become like Him.

"But many turn away from this concept because they always think of God in the negative. They greet Him each day pleading, 'Oh Great God, Maker of heaven and of earth, please hear me, this sinner. Though I have sinned against You, please forgive me.' They kneel or sit or stand with head bowed in abject humiliation. Never do they lift their heads to enter into real communion with this God to whom they take their prayers. They think of His greatness, and they think of their own poverty of spirit. Then they wait for blessings.

"There will be few blessings coming because those who stand with heads bowed do not think themselves worthy of blessings. They cannot believe that God loves them. They think they enter into God's presence by crawling to Him, and they believe God will be pleased at their humble attitude. But true humbleness is not this exterior position. Inside is what counts.

"Never come before God, however you think of Him, as a dishonest person who tries to beguile Him with an attitude of humility that may impress other people. God wants your honesty expressed, whatever it is. Therefore, come before Him with no thought of false truth which is much like the live sacrifice of old. This God of ours does not want live sacrifice. Abraham entered into that idea, but he learned that God does not expect such a thing. Therefore, give your true expression. Be the person you really are when you come to God. Be honest.

"God can then take you *where you are* and work through you and with you. Team up with the Brotherhood to learn how to make this idea into working power. We will help you tune in to the truth that will enter your mind to help you become the God-like person you want to be."

I mentioned that the Bible says that we should kneel before God. It also says we must confess our sins in order to be cleansed. Here is the commentary.

"The Bible explains humility here and there throughout, and it states that people should do this or do that in order to be tempered into God's people. The Bible has many words about approaching God because people had various personal experiences, and the writers wrote these down as valid for everyone. But the point we make over and over is that people must find their own way to become one with God as individuals. This, too, is in the Bible. But many believe there are certain universal steps that must be taken.

"We say, instead, that there must be recognition of the fact that God IS. That is all. Then the person must be absolutely honest in talking with God. God knows the thoughts, the inner feelings you have, so why try to be the fake person who uses ritual that isn't really believed?"

I questioned the meaning of the word "truth." Here is the Brotherhood's explanation about truth, what it is and how we determine it.

"The truth you speak of is hard to explain here. Truth varies from one to another because whatever we believe with all our hearts tends to be our truth. Therefore, what is truth? There are wars fought over truth, you know. There are new churches begun over the matter of truth. Therefore, to understand the word *truth* correctly, we must acknowledge that truth varies depending upon who expresses it.

"The *absolute truth* is that which the God of the Universe imparts to each individual, the truth that will help a person express an individual growth pattern in this lifetime. That's the way people grow. That's the way this reader will grow—by way of the truth imparted to him by God.

"Take the person who is writing this book, for example. This person, Jean Foster, will turn her mind now and then to the truth she has learned throughout the time she has been on earth. The writer gives her attention to the truth she has learned in study groups, in churches that preach truth, to books that express truth. Therefore, she is full of *truth.* But she knows nothing of her own truth, the truth that prospers her own soul, unless that truth comes to her through God-mind. Now is it clear what *truth* is?"

I answered that I apparently have a rich store of information *about* truth, but only recently have I begun to learn the truth that applies to my own soul's growth.

"That is the way it is with the reader, we suspect," the Brotherhood continued. "The reader comes to this book to learn *truth.* But instead, he learns that there is no such thing as *absolute truth* from outside sources. *Absolute truth* only exists in the inner person, that spirit self which is the reality of each of you.

"Therefore, to become the person who knows truth, it is absolutely essential to come to God who has your own truth stored away to be released upon your request.

"Team up with the Brotherhood of God to unite your mind with God-mind." Again the Brotherhood explained that it can accomplish this for us "because we have that eternal team of Brothers who want to give their own teamwork to help you. We will give the truth that will turn you to your great good. Most important, we will come to your aid when you ask us, and we will give you our great growth to use, to borrow, to employ on your behalf.

"Never entertain doubts. Any doubts you have must inevitably team up with other doubts to keep you from getting your heart's desire. They will teach you nothing, for they only feed on more doubt."

Puzzled at these words about doubt, I reminded the Brotherhood that an earlier paragraph said to be honest. Therefore, if we bring doubts to our counselor, aren't we merely being honest?

"Doubt teaches you that there is doubt," came the quick reply. "That's what we are saying. There is no way to overcome doubt to reach your mind unless you can rid yourself of doubt."

I inquired if doubt is the greatest obstacle to overcome before people ask the Brotherhood to help them. In their reply they used one of their many wonderful metaphors.

"This team will come to you when you ask even if you do doubt. However, doubt is like fog in the early morning. The fog is dense and you cannot penetrate it. Doubt is like that. There is no way to see through this doubt to the greatness that you can be."

I persisted in my questioning by noting that it seems easy to say that we in the earth life need to shed doubt, but just how are we supposed to do it?

"There will be no way to move forward if doubts are entertained. If doubt arises, a person can merely recognize it for what it is, the early morning fog. Within the mind a person can know that the fog goes away. To understand this, let us use an example. When you drive to work and there is a fog, do you turn on your lights and inch forward anyway? Or do you say it is hopeless to get to work and simply stay at home?

"To compare this example of fog to doubt, you can easily see that to go forward in this great search for truth, one must go forward even if doubt is there. However, the point is that doubt must not stop you from getting to your destination—personal truth. Nor does the fog stop you from going to work. You know that the fog will lift. And there must be this determination that doubt will fade away.

"Team up with the Brotherhood to make all doubt go away, for as you practice determination, doubt will leave. Then you will demonstrate this personal truth in your life, and you will know that God is all you hope He is. Enter into your inner temple. Invite the Brotherhood to enter also. Take us into your confidence. Be honest."

To help make this point clear about teaming up with the Brotherhood of God, I asked for an example of someone who experienced what they explained.

"We know a person who came to us in this way, doubting somewhat, but nevertheless determined to find her personal truth. Teaming up with us the best she could, in spite of that entering doubt, she began to hear this truth that was just for her. Her life began to get turned around into the kind of life she had always wanted. She turned herself into the kind of person who had power in her life because she practiced the truth she heard.

"Doubt simply faded away to nothing. There was only the pure energy of God there—that's all. No doubt remained as she began to demonstrate. That is what will happen to you as you practice entering into the temple along with us who team up with you to make your truth come to you.

"There has been more truth expressed today than most people have heard in their entire lifetimes," my communicator from the Brotherhood said, referring to this chapter. "Today we take this reader to the heart of the truth, to the entity which people think of when they think of God. Of course that entity only enters a mind to become what each person *thinks* God is.

"That entity that people conceive of as God is only the partial concept, of course, because no one can encompass the whole of God. God is more than any of us can comprehend. He is unlimited. Who can conceive of an unlimited concept? Who can conceive of an unlimited God entering your mind? The concept which people have is that which changes, of course, as they grow.

"This growth we speak of is that which happens to our spirit selves. This spirit that we are in reality takes its growth from God who presents the truth that a person needs. As that person then enacts the truth in his life, growth takes place. This is wonderful truth to understand. Accept this truth into your own life, for you will then not waste this lifetime of yours.

"Wasting a lifetime is a dismal experience, for when you come to this next plane of life, you will see with the perspective of spirit only. You will review your earth life and understand that you have either accepted the truth from God-mind to become the one you hoped to be, or that you refused it to become an inferior person.

"Now you are ready to enter into the next phase of truth. As you touch the truth of God-mind through that channel you team up with us to make, there enters the special personal truth which is yours and yours only to use for your growth. Take this truth to your heart and to your mind. As it enters, it will make new thoughts, new needs to take to the Brotherhood.

"The temple within you will be our meeting place where we will bring the truth to your mind. Be open to our message here. Be open to our help. Take this gift we offer you, this open channel that we can build from your mind to God-mind. Then we will be true partners.

"The gift that we bear to you is the good news that we can take God-mind truth to you. This gift is not wrapped in paper which will tear and turn into waste. It is not put into a beautiful vase or an attractive picture. These have their value, but they do not satisfy the soul forever. The gift we bring you wends its way through our minds, through our spirit selves, through the God power that we make use of.

"This gift is our own growth that works on your behalf. We here are skilled in this work we do with the Brother of Brothers, Jesus, and we know how to give you the help you need to make this lifetime all you desire it to be. Therefore, take this gift without fear, without thought of the cost. There is no idea of generosity here. This gift is given simply because it must be given. We want this thought understood. This is *not* generosity!

"This gift is the way we serve God who advances our own spirits to higher and higher levels of expression. This way the God of the Universe teaches us all simultaneously—you in the teamwork we bring you and we in the giving of our concepts of the God of the Universe. Growth comes to you in receiving, and it comes to us in giving. We all benefit. Enter into this work with us, understanding this teamwork that brings you into oneness with God.

"Think about this message, this understanding that our work with you is the best way that you can demonstrate God's truth in your life. This understanding will bring you into alignment quicker with our teamwork than if you hold the idea afar while you study it. Empty yourself of old truth and be open to new truth. This giving and receiving of truth empties the old truth into waste where it will run off as water runs off the roof.

"This way there will be no inner disturbance when your own personal truth enters you. There will be this wonderful entry of truth to overcome the old truth, to become the new growth in your spirit. This new growth is the real you, not the person you once were. Team your thinking with this idea of new truth and the elimination of old truth. This way the truth that your soul awaits will rush into you to become one with you.

"That you may better understand the truth we speak of, take this writer's truth that has helped her spirit grow. This writer has the personal truth that we helped enter her mind by way of God-mind through this writing. This truth told her that she is the person who has reentered earth life through an adult body. She has teamed up with us to make her goals work in this lifetime.

"That she entered life this way is not to be marveled at because there are many who do this. Perhaps you, the reader, have been one to enter life into an adult body. No one will ever take this person, this writer, to be other than the one who was born into this body because her body is still the same, her memories are the same, her responsibilities are the same. Even her loves are the same. Jean has not changed in her outer expression, but she has changed considerably in her inner being. Because her spirit entered this body, she became the writer who is part of this teamwork."

It's true that about six years ago my life underwent a change. I gradually developed better health, and I found greater joy in living. Situations that gave me problems resolved themselves because I took hold of them with new determination. I let go of feelings and attachments which bound me to the past, and I searched for ways to express my rising interest in abundant living. It's hard to express the change that took place, and it was not apparent to me that a new soul inhabited my body. Nor was it apparent to my husband. I only know that one day I felt stronger, more in charge. It was not until the Brotherhood and I were working together on our first book that I learned that this soul change had taken place.

"Never worry that a new spirit entity will disrupt the body," my spirit/counselor stated firmly. "Never worry that a new spirit entity will disrupt people's lives. This writer simply took the place of the former spirit, but she took on the same responsibilities. There has been a change, yes. This new spirit has taken the body to greater health, for one thing, and this entity takes the truth into her life to bring peace to her and to those around her. This spirit then takes on the truth project that she came to take on—the writing of this book, or series of books."

In "The God-Mind Connection," the Brotherhood explained this switching of souls. They said that when a person feels that he or she has reached the goals that were set for this lifetime, it is possible to retreat to the next plane of life and give up the body to another spirit. They characterized this giving up of the body as similar to giving up one's organs at death so that someone else may benefit. They said giving up one's body deliberately was superior to committing suicide, for this way the body is not wasted. All you need do, they explained, is to let the Brotherhood know that you are ready to give up your body to another spirit. Then if this change is for your spiritual good, the exchange will take place sometime when you are sleeping.

Did I specifically request this exchange? No, but my cries for help went out to God. The spirit self of my body was in despair, and life did not seem worth living. According to the Brotherhood I lay down for a nap one day, and when I awoke, the exchange was complete. When told of this exchange, I found it nearly incredible. Yet, I knew that I was a "new" person in many ways, and I had not been able to explain the many changes even to myself. I accept their explanation, as I accept the statement that the previous possessor of this body is happy that the exchange happened, and that she cheers me on. She goes on with her own life, I am told, though she is still helpful to Carl—her/my husband. I have no jealousy about her, only a feeling of loving cooperation.

"Each person who invites us," the Brotherhood continued, "will receive a way to team up with us to receive the truth of God. This truth enters, not to take over your life, but to enrich it. Truth will never 'take over.' There is nothing to fear from aligning yourself with God's truth. There will only be the good things of life for you, the truth that will take you from the slavery of unbelief to the freedom of belief. That is, you will go from the one who takes the truth of earth-mind, that collection of truths, half-truths and untruths that man collectively calls *truth,* to the God-mind, which is personal truth designed for your particular soul.

"Team up with us to be your very best self. Be unafraid in this. Take courage to your heart and take this truth to your mind. Between your heart and your mind, you will bring forth this new creation, this wonderful God-person that you are intended to be.

"Now take us at our word. Take this time to be the one who trusts in the Brotherhood whom Jesus works in and with.

Team up with us to make the truth you receive that which will bring you to entirely new thinking, entirely new living. Team up . . . team up . . . team up."

CHAPTER 6

GETTING THE MOST OUT OF LIFE

I want to live life to the utmost, but how do I claim this goal?

One morning as I sat at my typewriter ready to receive material for this chapter, my spirit/counselor from the Brotherhood let me know that I wasn't ready. "Go into your temple, and quiet your mind."

After a while I asked them to enter. Immediately they told me to throw all my negative feelings and thoughts to the wind. "The wind," the Brother told me, "will blow them away and God will remake them into fresh positive energy." I stepped to a window in my temple that overlooks a breathtaking view.

Mentally I threw all that was bothering me out that window where the wind caught it and took it far away. I didn't know I had so much to throw away. There were bags of material—words from another person, many, many words. I saw them blowing out across this splendor, and I was glad God could convert this trash to worthwhile substance. I even swept up the remaining few words from the carpet and dumped them out the window.

What valuable counselors these advanced spirits are! Unburdened, I could then receive the following material.

"Team up with the Brotherhood of Jesus Christ to enter the place where God will teach you the truth. Then your problems will lift from your shoulders, the giant outrage that encloses you in its vise-like grip will let you go free. Give your thought to us to become that total person, that potential which is what you want to become. Then your great character will emerge, and you will develop your talents.

"Many entities hold a limited concept of God. They believe that God will withhold the truth from them because they do not deserve it. They consider themselves unworthy, and they submit to the idea that God sends them suffering just to get them ready for greatness. What good heavenly Father would do these things?

"This poor concept of God makes people go to the door, so to speak, but not open it. They just stand there in the hope that God will break it down and grab them up, but they never grasp the handle or knob and pull the door open. There God stands to greet them, to give them the gifts of spirit. It is incredible to us in the Brotherhood that people would not open the door to receive God's good gifts.

"Be the ones to grasp the handle. Pull the door open. Then if you ask, the Brotherhood, inspired by Jesus, will give you the help you need to connect with God-mind. Join with us to bring yourself into this connection, into this wonderful presence of God Himself. Team up with the Brotherhood who stands here as the Counselor, the Comforter, the Holy Spirit who will give you all that you need to make that wonderful connection to God-mind."

At this point I received an introduction to a Brother who took over the writing to give specific information about spiritual growth.

"To help you understand the work of the Brotherhood, unite with me, the spirit entity who walked the earth with that Brother of Brothers, Jesus. The name I went by when I was in the earth life was Mark, the disciple of Jesus. I want to explain how the channel to God-mind works.

"To team up with our Brotherhood, you must have the pure thought that the Brotherhood does exist. Then when you become one with that idea, you can accept the truth that we bring through the channel that connects you to God-mind.

"This truth that pours into your mind comes straight from

God-mind, and it enters to help you to grow. It makes you a better entity, one who grows into a powerful spirit. Agree with this idea. Then when you have accepted it wholeheartedly, you can reach out for more truth.

"Tone the truth to your own spirit by working it through the mind that belongs to your spirit self. This truth will weld itself to you if you work to make it so. Throw doubt away. Turn your back on old truth. Then put this new truth into your soul where it will cling like it was the original part of you. Now you are ready to advance further.

"Turn yourself toward the gift of truth that we now offer you. When you have put sufficient truth into your soul, you can team up with the God of the Universe to build your own channel. There it will be—the understanding you need to put this channel directly into God-mind. The Brotherhood will rejoice, for it wants you to graduate from their teaching. They know when you make your own channel to God-mind, you will be all right on your own. Then they turn to others who may be reaching out feebly just as you once did.

"Growth sometimes goes slowly, especially if doubt persists in eroding the truth. But growth can go very fast when the mind and heart are open. But teaming up with this Brotherhood is the thing to do for all who feel uneasy, hesitant and doubtful. To those who believe but think they might be on the wrong track by themselves, we lend our assurance that all is well, that God is who He says He is.

"Understand that it is possible to build your own channel. Now you understand the spiritual goal we have here—to be one with God, you must become able to build your own channel."

I asked Mark what the difference is between going directly to God and building a channel to God-mind. He said, "The difference is that going to God directly means you *tell* God what is on your mind, but you seldom *listen* to Him. But when you go to God-mind, you expect to hear the truth that is best for your soul. When you go to God-mind, you may present needs, you may present goals, you may present all your hopes and dreams. But what you receive is the truth your own soul needs to make these things work out right in your life. Then you make use of the *absolute truth* from God, whereas going to God as you have done in the past only encourages you to retain the vague notion of who He is.

"There is one thing more on this subject. Teaming up with the Brotherhood is the surest way of going to God-mind to begin your truth work. Then you know that you progress when you can build this channel yourself. The Brotherhood is not jealous of your new abilities. Those in the Brotherhood only rejoice at your progress. Their work prospers when you go forward."

I asked why Mark was bringing this particular message. Perhaps this spirit who was Jesus' disciple in earth life has special knowledge?

"The particular truth that I bring into this book is the same truth I work with on this plane. My work here is with those spirits who team up with the Brotherhood to get help in building the channel from individual mind to God-mind. This work goes on all the time, but when people grow sufficiently, they move forward to the advanced level of building their own channels. Because I do this work, I see their growth. Be the one who moves forward in this way yourself.

"The entity who writes this book received the truth today that she is now ready to build her own channel directly to God-mind. She told me this idea wasn't the best one she has ever heard. But I insisted she is ready. Therefore, she shrugged mentally and told me she would go on with this. We in the Brotherhood think that we sometimes push her along, but since she is writing this book, she must enter into these experiences in order to be the best one to write of them succinctly.

"Be the one to now move forward. This work we do together here will help you to progress beyond your wildest imagination. Team up with me now to receive a message that will help you become one with the truth we give you here.

DEMONSTRATE YOUR TRUTH
by Mark

"Come into your temple where we will unite to bring you the truth of God-mind. Be into this channel building, either with our help or now on your own. Take this moment to sit there alone, thinking, teaming up with the Brotherhood, teaming up with God-mind. Team up . . . Team up to be one with the Brotherhood, one with the pure thought force from God-mind.

"Never doubt the existence of God-mind. This wonderful Mind turns to you night and day to tell you the truth you need and want. Your spirit self cries out for this *absolute truth*. Be into this adventure of going directly to God-mind. Team up with those who can help you to be one with this idea that God-mind will always give you the *absolute truth*. Give your own soul what it cries out for—truth that will help it to grow.

"Picture your spirit self going into your inner temple to enjoy what you have built and decorated. Belong to this place. Turn your head this way and that to enjoy this ornate beauty. Then enter the idea here that the God of the Universe wants you, His own child, to be the one who will turn to God-mind. Turn to this Mind by entering into that listening attitude the open channel provides. The Brotherhood will help you build this channel, but if you are ready, build it yourself.

"Give your attention to this channel. The thought flow then begins. Perhaps you have a pencil to record thoughts that come to you. Maybe you have a typewriter or even a word processor you can use. There may be some who hear the thoughts with their inner ears and can repeat them into a tape recorder. This method or any other method that will work is what we advise you to do. By making a record, you can go over it again, and then the words will stick in your mind.

"What I say here answers your practical need to understand how the truth gets to you and what it does for you. But there is more. Team up to understand how, when you once combine with the truth, you can enter the energy of God into your own being and make it work for you. This energy can produce thoughts in the physical world.

"But to command this energy, you must add certain things to the growth of your own spirit. First, you must believe that God has this energy in unlimited supply. Second, believe in this supply with the same fervor that you believe in the God of the Universe. By now you fully accept this unlimited concept of God, right? Finally, accept this simple thing—this idea that

God is the source of the energy that makes all things you see. It is this same energy that produces ideas, thought waves, and inspiration for people to use in developing their talents.

"The concept of energy is one you must consider fully and develop into the very fabric of your spirit. Otherwise you will not demonstrate this truth in your life. No way can you use what you do not even believe in. This is like the man and woman who love one another. The man loves this woman, but she cannot accept the fact of his love. He cannot point to love, nor can he weigh it out or describe it well. The man tries and tries, but she refuses to believe in this love. Therefore, these two people, who could have a good life together, separate. The woman could not believe in his love enough to make it become one with her spirit.

"It is the same situation when you combine the truth about the energy of God with your soul. If you deny it, or if you insist that there must be visible proof, you throw away the best gift God has for you. He stands there ready to present this gift, and all you need do is accept it. Why do you hesitate?

"This is my message to you, the reader. This is my own good news added to this chapter. This writing that opens your eyes to the possibilities of demonstration is the best that I can do. But no demonstration will happen unless you can accept my words wholeheartedly and make them part of your soul."

In this way Mark ended his message, and immediately a new messenger was introduced.

"Take time now to hear our good Brother, Enoch, who wants to bring you the next message. This spirit was the one who had his own temple on earth, the temple that brought him great fame and great power. But he wanted more than earthly power. He wanted spiritual power. Therefore, Enoch gave himself to the God he knew then, to his truth as he knew truth then. And when he teamed up in this wholehearted way, he experienced new thoughts, new experiences, new happiness. He then raised his conception of God to the unlimited and all-powerful God that he should not fear, but respond to with love. Then he united with those who talked to him from this next plane to teach him that the truth he wanted was still to come. Enoch opened himself to this truth to become the powerful spirit that wanted only to bring people to the same understanding he had about God. Now hear this spirit."

THE WAY TO BECOME ONE WITH TRUTH
by Enoch

"To become one with God we must be our true selves, not persons who unify with the present social order or who want power over others. To become God's own, you must let go of self, meaning you must let go of those thoughts that point you toward earth-mind thinking. This thinking only has a limited value because it will not last long enough for you to find the ultimate satisfaction you seek.

"Therefore, give your new thoughts to this God you know, and then let your mind open still further to the possibility of an even greater God. Believe this greater God wants to be your partner. Give this thought your greatest energy. Then you will be allied with the God of the Universe for sure.

"Teamed up with God, you cannot fail. Then you have power, great joy, wonderful freedom to be and to do whatever you wish. Can you think that big? Join with me, who is part of the Brotherhood, to let me help you open your mind. Give me your best thought on God. There! Think you want to know more? I hear your thoughts. Understand that I know you desire to make this growth.

"Give me your honest thought about what you want to be and to do. Again enter your temple with your goals, your dreams, your entire growth plans. We will go over these, you and I. Then we will lift them up to God by way of the channel that I will help you build to God-mind. Your truth center will take these goals and dreams into its concern. Now you will receive the truth that will show you how to accomplish them. Do not be afraid of all this procedure. There must be a procedure if you are to understand fully.

"People need a procedure they can understand. Simply *thinking* that you will give your goals to God may not be clear enough. 'How do you do this?' you think. 'How will I lift them? In a bucket, an elevator?' But God knows how hard it is for you in earth life to grab hold of abstract concepts; therefore, He teaches you by way of this Counselor, this Brotherhood. That is my message to you."

There are nine references to Enoch in the Old Testament in the book of Genesis, and there are four references in the New Testament. Enoch was named as the seventh generation after Adam, and he was the father of Methuselah. In Paul's letter to the Hebrews 11:5, he mentions Enoch. "By faith Enoch was taken up so that he should not see death; and he was not found, because God had taken him. Now before he was taken he was attested as having pleased God."

Following Enoch's message, my regular spirit/counselor again took over. "Team up to this tone of the Brotherhood, to this tone of pure thought. Give your *thoughtful* attention to our words here. Team up . . . This is the time for you to act in some way. Team up . . . Today you must take that step of growth. When you tender your thought to God, the truth that you need enters your mind. Then the truth becomes one with your soul. That is the plan. That is the eternal tender truth from God.

"Banding together with us brings you power because the Brotherhood holds the key to your soul growth. We understand your need to have an open channel to God-mind, and we provide you with that channel. Then you enter into the work of soul growth. The truth enters from God-mind, and it then teaches you what it wants you to understand. Then the partnership between us leads you into the demonstration of this new-found power. Get your thoughts in order. Get your goals established. Get the pure thought that you project in your mind to produce the things that you desire.

"Now, hold that thought in its reality in *whatever way is best for you*. The energy of the Universe that God will enter on your behalf will take this thought into reality. For some people this happens entirely too slowly, but for others it sometimes happens entirely too fast. The rate of producing thought into reality is governed only by your true understanding of how this wonderful energy works. You will get more control as time and experience teach you. Believe in this message, for without a demonstration, there will be no further hope of getting you to read the rest of this book, or of getting you to understand further truth.

"Believe in our work, the Brotherhood's work and in God's work. Believe, too, in your own ability to work this demonstration through. Team up with us to make this happen. Give it your total concentration. Give us your ear, your time, your entity who wants so much to become one with God and manifest the good thoughts approved by God.

"Team up to understand all that this chapter has brought to you. This chapter has not been easy, for it enters the earth scene to contradict what most people see in their experience there. But remember, this present earth life is only one experience out of many lifetimes. It is not the totality of life. The totality of life is the total experience which you, the spirit self, has had over eons of time.

"Our thoughts will be with you all as you work to grasp what we teach here. You have more help than you can imagine. God's spirits abound on this side, and they know how to help you. Teaming up with us will help you over the hurdles, take you to the core of the demonstration, reach the goals you have set. Team up, then, to arrive at your destination."

CHAPTER 7

GROWTH THAT NEVER STOPS

*I accept God truth. What more must I do to
live my life successfully?*

In the very beginning of my communication with the Brotherhood, the message I received over and over again was that "growth is everything." The statement sounded good to me. I believed in spiritual growth. But why, I wondered, did my counselors keep repeating it? I eventually came to realize that it takes a lot of spiritual work to combine with truth. Early on I thought that mental acceptance was enough, but the Brotherhood taught that growth is a constant process which is brought about through personal experiences. Even when you and I become one with the personal truth that comes to us through God-mind, we must protect it and nourish it. Otherwise, earth-mind truth weakens our growth.

The message from the Brotherhood came again as we began a new chapter. "The growth that never stops will combine with your spirit self and make you a new person. Give us your attention on this. The truth that comes to you through the open channel is your own truth, no one else's. Therefore, you will recognize it. Becoming one with this truth is your objective. Taming it makes it yours forever.

"Your growth is not limited any more than God is limited. It goes on and on, past your present earth life and on into more lifetimes. This growth continues to take you further and further into truth until you become one with God. When you attain this oneness, this perfect freedom of expression, you will become that which Jesus attained while on earth. Now turn your mind to us while we examine this concept further.

"Spiritual growth, which is your goal, will not take you to anything you do not want. Instead, it prevents you from wasting your life on earth-mind truth only. Give your attention, your open mind to the next concept.

"There is growth of spirit and there is truth that pours out on you but which does not adhere. This book, for example, can touch your life with truth and empty itself upon your soul. But if you turn your mind from it as it enters you, the truth will dissolve into the energy which brought it. Therefore, understand that you must reach out for this ongoing truth time after time, not just once.

"We will explain what mistakes you might be making. God-truth will never get to your soul if you deny it at the last moment. Denial will prevent you from taking the truth concepts to your inner being, to your truth center where you will make the growth happen."

The New Testament story about Peter denying Jesus came to mind. I asked if Peter's denial was like our own.

"The denial you speak of was Peter turning from the truth that Jesus gave him. Do not think Peter understood everything when Jesus was arrested. Peter was loyal, but he was also a human being who was afraid. In time Peter corrected his denial and took Jesus' truth into his own being. However, this story is not related to what we say here about truth. We will give you an example so you may understand the difference.

"Jesus, the teacher, gave truth to people in person, and some believed and some did not. But the truth *we* speak of is that which has always been available to people when they turn to God. Sometimes this truth comes in a visible form, sometimes it comes as sound, and sometimes it is intuition. But it always comes.

"Though truth has always been here for people, they put this truth into their minds just so far and no farther. All this kind of thinking does is to temporarily inspire; it does not result in permanent growth of their spirit.

"Jesus gave a parable about truth falling on rocky ground, right? Then he said this truth entered people, but it did not last because they did not take care of it. Only those who were good gardeners, so to speak, got the benefit of truth. Therefore, that is what we say now, to you, to your inner being. This truth that will adhere to your very soul and promote growth must be invited, must be presented to your inner self, must be watched over while it grows to be part of you."

My next question concerned what you and I are to do in watching over this truth. Here is the answer.

"This watching is not as difficult as many imagine it to be. The truth that you have wanted and waited for spills over you. When you understand it, the truth may change your whole life around. Will you accept that change? Will you nourish the truth that obviously means you will give up many things while you take on other things? This truth will change your very core. Will you take these changes in stride?

"Now you see what we mean when we tell you that truth sometimes does not last even though you have opened your mind to it. No one who wants truth will be denied. But those who accept truth and enter it permanently into their growth are those who go the extra mile, so to speak. They will team up with the Brotherhood to help them hold and keep this truth emptying into them. They will rid themselves of their doubts and fears in order to make way for this new growth. They step forward in their conviction that God IS, that Jesus IS, and this team of Brothers/Counselors IS.

"Team up with the thought we give you here, or else the truth that pours in to your inner self may spill upon the ground and flow away. Now you must understand. The Brotherhood is firm in its dedication to help you go beyond the point of simply receiving truth. We want you to understand that the truth you accept into yourself is that which makes you grow, not that which you simply hear or read.

"Here is another point. Watch the hands on a clock. They move ever so slowly to measure the time, but if you join our team, these hands will seem to swing furiously around the clock. This better view of our powerful energy may be shown by the hands on the clock. There is no wasting the truth when this happens. Time seems to flow along with greater speed when the powerful energy of God has hold of you.

"You will team up with this energy to enjoy life more, to become one with truth. No one will be able to wrest this glorious truth from you because you have it as you have the skin on your body. This powerful truth will take you to new ideas, new places, new energy that will turn your life into the newness you want. Then the truth you wear like skin will become the integral part of your soul, and you will then operate your life with this truth. Team up with us to enter this truth we give you.

"The truth that you wear like the skin on your body will become a permanent fixture in your soul *as you use it.* Only then will you become new. You will no longer be the same person who *tried* to be open to truth. You will then *have* it.

"Now take another idea into your mind. Hold the thought of this accomplished growth. You are a new person, so to speak. You are ready to turn to God-mind again for more personal truth. From this point on you will be led to more ideas, more concepts that you have not considered before. Again upheaval returns to your life because new truth calls for change. But the change is not catastrophic. It is that which brings you further growth. That's the way it goes, step by step.

"The growth of your soul never stops. It goes forward to still more growth. Then one day you become one with God, and you know then how to be the potential that God has always intended you to be. We speak here to your spirit self, not the body. That you may become your potential in this one lifetime probably is not possible. Nevertheless, there will be more good come to you in this one lifetime than you can even imagine when you become one with the truth that will help you grow.

"New persons—those who accumulate new growth—put their truth into expression because they simply cannot help it. The irresistible urge to express is there. There is no way to be the dull person you once were, the one who looked out at life afraid of what might happen if you did this or that. Be the person it is possible for you to be. Be that one who accepts the truth that is here for you, the truth that will enter you to become the growth you need to perform in this lifetime with all the greatness and energy that is possible.

"Be the one to perform the tasks that others think are impossible. Be the person who others say it is not possible to be. Take the truth into action to perform that which others say is too hard or impossible. Be the one to enter into the Brotherhood to team up with us. Enter the temple of your inner being where we will help you become the one who is invincible.

"New growth comes to those who seek it. This is the rule or the law that is entered into the book of books—that which is written by God Himself. Other laws are, 'New growth is to be used,' and 'No one who seeks God will be denied access to Him.'

"Give your thought to the concept of God as the team who plays the game. You watch this team perform for awhile, but then you decide you would like to participate. You call on us to coach you in becoming a good player. This way we all work to win the game of becoming one with God. This concept is easy to understand, is it not?

"This wonderful God, who works continuously to perform the team's good, will make you part of His team. Be the one who does more than sit in the stands watching. Be even more than the one who sits in the stands cheering. Be the one to take yourself onto the field, so to speak, where the action is. There is a reward—the wonderful growth that you will enjoy. This growth puts you on your way toward the ultimate goal of being one with the great God of the Universe who is the Goodness, the Mercy, the Ultimate Concept of what is beautiful, what is best and what is perfect.

"Take all of this chapter to your mind, please. Then you and we will progress to our next step, whatever that is. That step depends on where you are in spirit development. But wherever you are, we are there with you to help you in this wonderful growth that is yours merely for the seeking."

CHAPTER 8

INVITING TENDERNESS INTO YOUR LIFE

Is there some way to attract true friends and a true mate?

Three universal truths, all of which deal with tenderness, are presented in this chapter. Tenderness, according to the Brotherhood, is that which joins our spirit to God's.

The first truth presents a caring God who understands and fills our needs. The second shows us how we can find friends in our earth life who are spiritually tuned in to us. The third reveals a way to determine who is our true and compatible mate.

The material for the first universal truth comes from one Brother who read from an ancient manuscript that was written when the Jews were on their way to the Promised Land. "The truth that we present here is the basis for this chapter. This section on tenderness is to remind people that God is not the far off unattainable spirit that wafts Himself into the high heavens away from the practical affairs of earth life. God enters into the affairs of men and women when they open themselves to Him.

"Join with us to learn how this God of the Universe presented great truth in the early days of truth-giving. God wanted His people—those who gave their spirits and their time to His truth—to open themselves to great truths about Him. Therefore, He wrote on these matters through the men of the time. These enlightened messengers wrote faithfully what God put into their minds. But when the truths were handed to others, they took them only as interesting thoughts, not concepts to make their own. This truth helped people understand that God wanted them to be His family. But they thought they were the *one and only* family God had in mind. They turned the truth on its head, you see, and they missed the entire point.

"Now we must get to the heart of the matter. Open your mind. The God of the Universe gave His good to the people on the earth plane. They did not understand all they received because they thought that the God of the Universe was the One up in the sky somewhere. They did not accept God as even being interested in their problems of survival, their problems of getting to the Promised Land.

"Here is what the God of the Universe wrote for them: 'Take the message that I give to you, the children I love, to enter it into your hearts and minds. The God you worship is the same God who will bring you the truth you need to make your journey to the Promised Land. This truth will give you the entry to hope, to the good that I have ready for you. But you must write these truths on your soul so that you will act in accordance with all I give you.

" 'The truth that you need now is that which will bring you safely through these times and into the time to follow. This truth will then give you all that you hope for and desire in that new place. Team up with this thought, this truth, this message that I bring you through this writer. This entire truth is to give you all the power you need to enact your good.

" 'Give your attention to me, to My good truth. The God that I AM is the same God that each one of you IS. The God that I AM enters each of you to team up with you to express all the powerful teaching that I give here. This truth enters you to say that we enter into this lifetime expression together, so you know you are not alone. Therefore, team up with me to know that we undertake to enter the Promised Land together.

" 'Now give your attention to the truth that people need to understand. To enact this great twosome enterprise, we must work together in a partnership that begins now and will never end. This partnership begins with your becoming one with the truth that what I say is true, and it never ends because there will be a relationship between us that is unbreakable.

" 'Take yourself now to the next idea I present to you. Be into the *entire* truth, for to try to make yourself one with only the first is to make yourself a wagon without wheels. This wagon will go nowhere. But with the wheels there is the potential to go anywhere. Therefore, take *all* this truth into your being.

" 'Give your heart to me—your emotions, your tenderness, your love, your great open warmth. These emotions will bring us into our best enduring relationship because these are the qualities of true friendship. This way you will have the enduring Friend, the One Who will never desert you, Who will be there with you forever. This truth means that you will always have these warm feelings with you. There will be no emptiness within you, no unfulfilled longings, for I AM there. This is my pledge to you, the people whom I love.' "

Cynics may ask if that ancient manuscript was written in English. My counselor from the Brotherhood explains about the language. "The manuscript was written in the script of that day. Those who were schooled in Egypt brought their skills with them, and they were the ones to make the words on the parchment they had then. These thoughts were put into the words of that day and that time, but they would make no sense to you. Therefore, we brought the truth behind the language, in thought form, and this writer puts them into the only language she knows, English. That is always our procedure. There is no language on this plane, only thought. Communication is hard to explain to you on the earth plane, but when you team up with us on the personal level, we will bring you the truth from God-mind in thought form.

"Team up with us to know that God had these truths in mind from the beginning of His relationship with mankind, who changed these truths to suit others. Therefore, much that was not from God crept into the books of the Pentateuch (the first five books of the Old Testament), and thus began a series of errors in thought.

"These truths are important, for many of you reading this

book recognize them as the ones that God speaks to you either now or in a past life. Therefore, you respond to this truth with your whole being. This great truth is more than we alone can bring you. You must know it comes to you through this writer to whom we read this manuscript. Take this to your heart, dear reader. These truths are the eternal ones that will change earth life for you and for many.

"The truths that bring you good friends and your true mate come through God-mind to help each of you live your lifetime in great happiness. The truth that God cares about you is what this chapter is all about. God of the Universe, all powerful, will tend to your individual needs to help you prosper in all ways. There is the miracle, if you want to enter into miracles. The God of the Universe who is the One who has the entire universe to tend, still cares for you, and you and you, too.

"All of you want to bring people into your lives who will prosper you in every way. As you learn how to use the universal energy, you will bring those people into your life who belong there. They will find you irresistible when you accept this truth and enact it.

"There is no way to tell which person you meet is on your tone or energy pattern. However, teaming up with this truth we give you now will make this tone evident. Therefore, bring your open mind to this wonderful truth.

"The tone you have is unique. It can, however, combine with other tones which have certain similar tensions. But it is hard to tell from your perspective which persons have these tones that combine well with your own. Take this message to heart. Take the energy that comes through God-mind to your mind now. Think of yourself as spirit, for that is your reality. Then be into the tone by taking your own personal thought that you put out toward other people. What is this thought? Team up with this now. Let your mind cooperate.

"Now hold this thought that usually passes through your mind when you meet others, either those you know well or those you meet for the first time. Hold this thought out to them. To do this, think of this certain person whom you know. Then hold the thought that comes to your mind about this person.

"Give your thought to the person. Then wait. After a while, mention the person by name. Give this message to the person as if he were standing in front of you. 'Team up with me, (name), to be the friend I want and need in my life.' Then mentally take that person's hand and wait. Now, take this picture you have of the person and let it energize by putting your entire thought into it.

"This process is something like taking a picture with a camera, only your private temple is the developing room, so to speak. The picture is taken with your spiritual eyes, the ones that see more clearly than the body's eyes. The picture is taken, held in your mind, then energized by God's own energy and developed. When at last you see that picture come forth, hold it in your hands. This picture is the true picture of the person you think you might like for a friend.

"The picture that you hold in your hand does not feature only body characteristics. Therefore, you see this person clearly, not a picture that earth-mind develops. Team up with us to know if you want to be a true friend of this person. To merge into our truth, open your mind now. Work with us. Become one with the truth that we bring you. This is the way to know whether or not the person may become the true friend you are seeking.

"Earth-mind will tell you to make friends with all kinds, but God-mind tells you to temple only with those who temple well with you, those whose tone or character meets the requirements needed to become one with your tone. Why is this method better than the earth-mind method? Teaming up with others who have no qualities like your own will make a poor friendship or a poor marriage. With the wrong friends or mate you will not be the truly fulfilled person you long to be.

"These relationships that we have in each lifetime are the ones that either prosper us on our way to meet our goals, or they are the ones that deter us from our goals. That these friends may or may not hurt us is not the point. The good friends in earth-mind context will be there for you through the good times and the bad, but they will not be able to give you much strength to help you through.

"Now turn your mind to the templing procedure with which

we began. Templing with other people on the spiritual level will take no more time than the earth-mind method of getting to know them through several meetings. New partners will enter your life when you use this God-mind method, for they will be drawn to you irresistibly. Now heed this: energize the thought when you think it. It may be a question, perhaps, or a wondering about the person or some reaction to the other person's posture or touch."

Is there some kind of example from earth life that we might relate to, I asked. "Teaming up with this method will take you to the best of mates, for example. There is much 'falling in love' in the earth life, but there is not much in the way of getting God-mind truth to enlighten you about this person.

"That's why there is so much divorce. People pick persons and go with that person for years without measuring the tones. But this can be done when people first meet. That's the way to avoid the mismatching that does individuals harm.

"Teaming up with this truth will open your eyes to the people in your life today who may bring you present joy but who will not last the time through. This way, the way of taking this truth into your inner being, you will avoid the possible heartaches that come about because you have made the wrong associations."

I asked if by this method we pronounce judgment upon others, and the Brotherhood said that "this is not judgment in the sense of calling people bad or good or saved or unsaved! This truth enables us to know our own tone, our own character. Then we can team up with others who are compatible with this inner person who is our reality. Our goal here is to teach you there in the earth plane to know how to team up to this truth so you can bring entities into your life who should be there."

What about the people who are already in our lives? Can we use this universal truth to evaluate our relationship?

"We can use this method to find out why relationships do not seem to be working. This procedure will tell us why, for example, the child and the parent do not get along. We enter this idea to give you some insight into your problems with others, not to get you to abandon your responsibilities, however. This insight should help you to team up with us to get the help you need to give this person in your life whatever is needed. But it will also teach you that the closeness you expect may never come. This way you do not become disappointed or morose over a poor relationship with someone you think should be close to you.

"This truth method enters into a person's own consciousness to give perspective that comes from God-mind. Use this truth to evaluate each relationship, if you wish, and then go to God-mind for further truth, not to other people. These friends or this mate you have now, who may not team up well with you, will nevertheless remain part of your life until the truth manifests. This means that when you become one with this truth about bringing the right people into your life, then the right people will inevitably come. The others may stay, but they will have no power over your life to make it happy or unhappy.

"Never assume that people are what they promise with their faces and their touch. They may not be sincere, and you can always tell the deeper self when you follow the procedure we gave you. Take that first thought to your inner self where you will let God touch up the picture which will then tell you if you will be compatible with this person.

"Now work with us in another way. Let us concentrate this truth upon choosing the right mate. To be a happy wife or a happy husband, take this new truth to heart. Take us to your mind now and to your heart, too.

"You will want to find a husband or a wife to team up with who has the same purpose and goals that you have. But this purpose will not be realized, nor will the goals be met if the the husband or wife take their partners without the necessary compatibility.

"Team up with us to become one with the truth that you can choose the right mate. Here is the way it is done by God-mind truth.

MEDITATION TO FIND THE TRUE MATE

"Enter into your own inner temple. Get into a comfortable position; send your thought toward the truth that enters here.

Now you are ready. Be into this attitude that *now you are ready*. Take the light that streams through the window into your own being.

"Now enter the picture of this person whom you believe you want to marry. Team up with this picture to the point that it enters into the very design of your temple. Then hold yourself in position to enter into this picture.

"Take a step toward the picture. Take the next step until you walk right into this picture. Then hold yourself there while the truth of God-mind enlightens you.

"This picture, which is your proposed partner, will combine with your own spirit or it will not. If you feel resistance there, a desire to separate into two persons, then this perfect templing of your two spirits will never occur. But if you think this picture you hold is the one you want to enter into, to become one with, and it happens while you hold it in mind, then take this person for that mate who will temple with you for your lifetime."

In rereading this meditation, I thought perhaps the attraction to the picture depended too much on emotions. I asked if sexual attraction alone could be responsible for wanting to become one with the other person.

"This won't happen because the picture you hold in your inner temple becomes spirit even as you are when you enter your temple. That you would still want to be sexually entwined in this temple when you are both spirit is not likely. This way of bringing the two of you together in the temple which is for spirit-entities only will be the way to truly evaluate your templing possibilities.

"The picture you bring to your inner temple must contain what you see in that person. No way will this picture remain perfect while in your temple. The entity has growth needs. That is why he or she is here in this earth life. Therefore, this person that you see will be the one *who is*, not the one who wanders the earth pouring an earth personality upon others and expecting to be judged by what others see and touch. The picture on earth is one thing, but in spirit it is something else. That is the way it is with us all.

"You may think that templing with a picture is somewhat strange. But the picture is only a symbol to use. The reality is the spirit of the intended mate. When you see that reality, then you will decide in spirit form whether or not your two souls will be good for one another. The entire point here is that you do not look at profession, at outer countenance, at an entire physical review; you must go to the spirit self.

"Teaming up with only part of this truth will not manifest results. The truth has an open channel to put you in touch with it. To understand whatever you need to, put yourself in touch with God-mind who will explain it all just for you in terms that you will accept and use.

"Now give your open mind to us again to receive still another idea about how to attract the right person to be your friend or to be your true mate. If you will empty your own sense of ego to let the God of the Universe express through you, you will be irresistible to compatible ones. Think, *'Open my mind to you, oh God, the One who empties His truth upon me now.'* This will tell the God of the Universe you are ready to become one in this matter of understanding your own truth.

"Then wait until your mind is still and quiet. Take time to do this regularly. Now open your eyes to the advanced spirits who will help you in the expression of God's truth within you— the Brotherhood who walks with you when you invite us. We will be there in that moment to help you express your own personal truth from God which will make you irresistible to those persons whom you want in your life.

"Put yourself into our hands here. Team up with us now. We will take our good measure of you to know how to best help you. But together we will attain those relationships you most want—the loving and true relationships that make a lifetime the wonderful warm experience it should be.

"We want you to understand how compatibility works. Every person has a tone that is special or unique. It will not be the same as anyone else's. Never think that two persons can be one or will occupy the same space, for this is not possible. But there can be compatibility. Never open the other person's energy to you or your energy to him unless you are sure of compatibility."

The Brotherhood refers to tone, or character, in terms that I identified with radio frequencies. I asked for a comment. "This tone is wonderful in that it expresses you in spirit form without energy from anyone else. The tone is that which invites expression. It is hard to explain because our plane is all spirit, and this tone is very natural. In your plane it is not entirely the same.

"The tone is spirit, certainly, but it is not the physical part. Therefore, you cannot see the tone; you can only sense its presence. But do not worry. Each person has an inner knowledge when he meets someone whether or not this person is possibly compatible. But what we give you here will take the question away and create the certainty.

"Then you can gather your forces and concentrate on those individuals who will be your own personal friends because they become what they innately are—compatible with your tone, your inner vibration center. The vibration center is not like radio waves, however. The vibration center is based on each entity's own wonderful or not so wonderful expression of truth. There it is."

Just how essential, I wondered, are these compatible persons to our successful life and to our spiritual growth.

"Team up with us to understand their importance. The entities in life expression—you—who become one with this truth will form attachments quickly that will truly help them to grow in this lifetime. But those who wander from one to another in earth life will not grow as fast because they concentrate so on these poor relationships.

"Take marriage, for example. This relationship can use up energy that will take them to no point whatsoever if the mate is not compatible. Poor relationships will often destroy a person's life experience, and that individual will waste it completely. Be a person who wastes nothing that will contribute to your spirit growth. Be into these truths we offer that you will most likely succeed with your life's goal.

"Go now to your truth center. Take this center you have built inside you, this gorgeous temple that is ornate and perfectly lovely. Take the time to enter there with your own perfect image of the truth we give you. Now enter this truth into the spirit that you are. Take it to the mind; take it to the heart. Team up with it perfectly.

"But when you leave your temple, take your truth with you and practice it in your life experience. What is revealed there will team up with you to help you find those persons in your life who will be the tender warm presences who will enrich your life as you will enrich theirs.

"Use this truth that is present for you. Hold it close to your heart. Do not fear losing friends or husband or wife. Those people whom you lose will be the ones who would have never come so close into your life if you had practiced the truth that we give you now. This way you will welcome only those whose tone is compatible with yours, you see."

If your marriage flounders, is this the procedure to use to find out if your mate is really right for you?

"In each instance team up with us. Then apply the truth procedure we gave you. There, in your inner temple, with the picture of this person with you, we will help you see your mate with eyes that see past the physique, the smile and the touch. We will help you deal with this entity on the spirit level. This is how you will know whether a poor relationship is due to some unkindness or to basic incompatibility. This is important to know. But you will never understand this if you cannot enter this truth into your mind now.

"This team of Brothers gives its energy to you when you accept it. This new energy we can give to all who ask, to you when you want it. It will help you become the kind of person you want to be—irresistible to those whom you wish to attract. This truth we bring you that your life may be happy and filled with loving warm presences."

CHAPTER 9

PUTTING ENTHUSIASM INTO YOUR LIFE

How can the Brotherhood help people develop enthusiasm?

The Brotherhood of God says that if we are to understand clearly how to live our lives with great enthusiasm, we must understand the difference between universal and personal truth. "Personal truth," they explain, "is that which we receive from God-mind directly." This truth is entirely our own, designed for our particular soul growth. "Universal truth," they say, "is intended to be useful to all regardless of individual differences."

According to the Brotherhood, "To get enthusiasm, one must team up with the truth that God-mind brings. This will not be universal truth; it will be personal. Therefore, there is *no* way we can team up with the readers as a group to teach them how to bring enthusiasm into their lives. You must receive the personal truth from God-mind through the open channel. Then, and only then, will enthusiasm become a reality in your life expression. Joy will arise from within you, and it will be everlasting because it is one with your spirit.

"This is our best chapter, we think, because there are so many of you who lose your enthusiasm for living for one reason or another. There must be enthusiasm for life or there is no teamwork to accomplish your goals. By this we mean there is no person who can go his way alone in earth life. Teaming up with others is needed—teaming up with us, teaming up with the compatible people in your life, teaming up with the God of the Universe through us or through your own channel building.

"Teaming up is our way of giving you the truth that your soul needs and requires. This teamwork is personal, of course, as we have told you over and over, and it is always there whether or not you take it. Therefore, the enthusiasm we speak of is what is needed in earth life to enable you to reach out to take hold of the truth we offer.

"Giving up—the opposite of enthusiasm—is what makes teamwork come to a standstill. But this standstill need not be permanent if you know what to do to get things moving. The truth we give is always there for you, and we come at your bidding through the door of your temple, the door you built there just for our entry. We will enter fast, and we enter joyfully as always.

"Therefore, take this message to heart. Giving up comes about when life overwhelms you. But this need not happen when you take your life in bits and pieces. This is the way to attack your problems, one by one. Take your work, for example. Perhaps you find your work hard beyond belief, or dull beyond belief or outrageous beyond belief.

"Team up with us to implement changes that will make your job situation different and better than it is now. Take this job into your inner temple where we all are. Make yourself comfortable there, and invite us to hear you out. We will come to you with smiles and reassurance. Now tell us your problems. Talk out loud if you wish. Be the one to team up with us in the truth we bring.

"Now that you have told us all about your job, we will offer our own suggestions. Focus your attention on our entire opinion. Then we will connect you with God-mind to let the absolute truth that is just for you flow through to you. Hear it within you or sit down as this writer does and write or type it out as you enter it into your mind.

"Take the truth that has come to you and act upon it. This may mean going into some new work, and you will have to make proper use of this truth to do what it suggests. But if you

turn aside because you fear change, then your problem is not
the job, it is fear of change that is wrong in your life. Be alert
to these clues into your very nature. Then you and we must
talk about what bothers you most—fear of change. Do you see
how this works?"

I asked about an acquaintance who is given to deep depression. Physically she is all right, according to her doctors, and
she is not sure what causes her depression. I asked the Brotherhood how this system they describe could work for her.

"This person must start at the beginning of this book. When
she takes the truth step by step, then she will know what is
wrong in her life. She can pinpoint it somewhat to help us
counsel with her. Perhaps she will say that she is dissatisfied
with her life, that she seems to have no purpose for living.
Then she can turn to us with this idea.

"We will listen to her express this desperate situation. Then
we will help her pinpoint the actual problem. 'Now,' we will
say to her, 'turn your mind inward, inward to your own being.
What do you see there?' She may answer, 'hopelessness.' We
will then enter closer to her to connect her with the God-mind
truth which will pour through our channel into her mind.

"This person will then say, perhaps, that she entered life to
be this wonderful person, this marvelous wife and mother. But
now there is nothing. We enter this great truth to her that
tells her what her real mission on this earth is, what her plan
is. 'Why,' this truth may tell her, 'you did not come just to do
those things. Energy awaits you to become even more than
that. Why do you enter into the idea that you can do no more?
Why do you not team up with this truth that comes to you?'

"This truth will speak to her soul most privately. When she
withdraws from her inner temple, she will know there is more
to life than what she had supposed. She will look around her,
opening her eyes. But she will come again and again to her
inner temple to ask for her truth, and entering this temple
will energize her being daily or even more often until she
looks out at life with new energy, new enthusiasm.

"This inner working is the solution to all of life's problems,
you know. The truth that enters this person will reactivate her
understanding of her plan, her very own indescribably joyous

plan that she came to earth to carry out. When she gets this picture in mind, her depression will fall away as an entire shell. This person will then enter into life renewed.

"There is much, much more to this chapter before we close on the matter of this amazing energy that comes to put enthusiasm into your life experience. Be into this truth that undoubtedly astounds you with its promise. But do not turn away from it, or you turn away from the gold mine that you can use to prosper your life.

"Now understand this truth as it pertains to the most excellent prospect of all—putting your growth plan into perfect execution. Why not put it into perfect execution? Your soul will not be satisfied with less, will it? After all, you have been living lifetime after lifetime to bring growth to your soul. This is how growth is accomplished, by putting your plan into perfect operation. Therefore, why be satisfied with anything less than this goal?

"Team up with the Brotherhood that Jesus himself inspires, leads and energizes. Though doubt is natural, acceptance of our miraculous energy is what you must strive for. Understand? This truth will make a difference in your life. Therefore, doubt it if you must, but do not let it fade away because you need what it will bring you.

MEDITATION TO HELP YOU UNDERSTAND

"Now open your eyes and your heart to your inner self. Go into your temple again. Be into an attitude of quiet. Then invite us in through this side door. We come there to you with smiles and excitement because you stand ready to accept still another truth into your mind. Now listen.

"The truth you receive opens your eyes to the possibility of becoming what you want to be. What is it? Enter this picture of what you want to be into this slot of time. Combine this picture with your own spirit entity. Enter yourself into the goal you have. There! Can you open your mind to this? If not, try again. Take your time here. Take your entity, your spirit self which we know is of God, and put this spirit self right in this beautiful temple which you have already built. Enjoy your temple. Focus on its various aspects of beauty before you invite us in to share it with you.

"Give yourself a picture of the person you would like to be. Put this picture in your mind. The picture is yours, no one else's. That is, it is no one else's unless you have entered someone else's picture there. Look—have you entered the picture of someone else—someone whom you admire, perhaps? This picture will not do, for we cannot make use of the picture of another. Turn to your own picture. Let it rise up from the depths of your mind where you put those dreams that you have of life and attainment. Team up with the mind that you have. Team up with those deeply hidden dreams you have. Team up with them so that they rise to the surface.

" 'Oh,' you may say. 'This dream is rather much at my age, isn't it?' Well, let's look at it. How is it too much? Enter your objections. We will then look more closely at it. Then you will either revise or you will hold to it. 'Well,' you may say, 'here it is. You told me to drag this great dream of mine out into the open. Now what do I do with it?'

"Why, we tell you, this dream is perfectly wonderful. Why don't you work on it?

" 'But I'm too old to start something new,' you may protest.

"Nothing is too hard for the one we take to our wonderful teamwork. No one is too old or too young; no one is too feeble or too uncertain of himself.

" 'The things I need to do to accomplish this seem too great,' you may say to us.

"Be the person God wants you to be, we say. We will help you in all things to make this dream come true.

"Because we talk to each person, we can work in an individual way to persuade or to enlighten. The sample conversation we gave is just that—a sample. It is not your conversation because you are a special person, and we will speak to you as you, not as to a big group."

Many readers may be asking, "Is it really possible to speak to the Brotherhood in this straightforward way?" I asked the Brothers if they would like to comment on this question, and here is their answer.

"This conversation is possible and most likely if the reader has read the book up to this point and has tried to become the one to put the truth we have given into his being. But we will enlighten the reader even more on this way of conversing.

"Be into the temple of your being. Have you built that temple detail by detail? Have you brightened it? If not, let us enter there together, we through your side door and you however you usually come. There we are looking over this temple. There are some places that need brightening, we see. There! We throw gold and silver brighteners into those dark places. How do you like that sparkling effect? It is quite beautiful, we think. We can do more if you want us to do so. Therefore, watch us and tell us if you want us to act to enlarge the temple or to brighten it in any way.

"While we are there together, tell us what you want us to do. Can you hear us when we speak? Can your mind feel the words we think toward you? Perhaps you want to write or type as this writer does. We will work with you however you wish. This way we will promise you the conversation you want.

"Team up with us to improve your communication skills. We enter into this work with several possibilities, and we work with each person to find the entry that works well. With this writer, we entered into her open mind while she told us her energy problems. Wending our thoughts to her, we communicated in writing, first by pencil, then by typewriter and now through a computer word processor. That may please you, too. It may not. The method is not the important thing. Communication is the important thing.

"Tend to your own self in this matter of communication. Enter into this communion we have in your inner temple. Enlarge this communication so you may receive the counseling and guidance through God-mind that we can connect you to. This is our goal.

"Now we will go on to the matter of the enthusiasm that comes to you when you put us into your life in the way we have outlined. The entry we make into your life will create thoughts within you that will lead to encouragement about your goals and ambitions. The entry will also take you into the truth that will temple with your growth center or soul. Then this enthusiasm will be yours.

"There will be within you the assurance that you enjoy the fellowship of true believers—this Brotherhood. The enthusiasm you receive through the application of this truth to your own being will take you into the best lifetime experience you can now imagine. Enthusiasm in life is a secret force, you know. It is your truth in action to become the realization of goals and potential.

"Reconsider the life you now live and the way you combine with the truth. Is it complete? Is it the best it can be? Do not take the truth from individuals who offer only their truth, for you will receive only a temporary experience, not real fulfillment. Consider only the hope we bring you—not empty hope, but hope based on God Himself. There is no experience to equal that of being teamed up with the truth of the God of the Universe.

"Now let us point out the pitfalls that you might find at this point. No one else must enter into your personal truth because the other person may dissipate it. Other people cannot understand your truth, you see, because it is not for them. Therefore, they may ridicule your truth or try to water it down. They may point out your terrible temple and tempt you to take it away or to tear it down. Also, they may encourage you to team up with earth-mind, which people may find more acceptable than the individual truth that comes from God-mind. Team up with the understanding we give here, or you may lose the best opportunity of your life—this lifetime, anyway.

"Now that we have shown you how to enact the truth to temple with enthusiasm, there must be this addition. *More of your time must be spent in your temple than you have spent heretofore.* This temple must be your place of rest and nourishment. Combine this idea with your truth center, that you and the temple you have built are now a permanent part of you, the part that will bring you the truth from God-mind.

"Team up with us to become one in spirit, that is, in desire and in the search for and the receiving of God-mind truth. Team up with us in this most valuable work because there is no other way to enter into a life that is enthusiastic and joyful. Be your own best sculptor here. Team up with us to mold your life experience into that which is truly wonderful and magnificent. This is our own message, our own best truth.

"This ends the chapter. Take these words to your inner temple, work with them yourself and put them into your truth center so that you may have this great enthusiasm for life."

CHAPTER 10

TONE, TENSION AND TRUTH

How does the law of attraction work?

In chapter eight, "Inviting Tenderness into Your Life," the words tone and tension were used, but they were not explained in detail. Therefore, the Brotherhood wants now to give a more detailed explanation of these and tell you that both tone and tension are in your hands and yours alone. God will not, cannot, change your tone or undertake the proper tension. The Brotherhood can, however, help you to understand and know your own tone. Then as you, and you only, decide to change it, they can help you to do just that.

"Team up with us to understand the tone of our souls. This tone we all have is the part of us that gives out a vibration to the other tones in the universe. The individual tone is unique, but it can team up with the vibrations of other entities who enter this person's field of energy if the tones are compatible. No one knows of this tone overtly, but each spirit entity has a tone nevertheless.

"Team up with us to understand this matter. If the vibrations you have are compatible with our own, we can work together very well. Teaming up is, therefore, very easy. But when the vibrations do not mesh well with our own, we use our good teamwork to unite us in spite of our differences. This adjustment works from the Brotherhood to individuals, but if the tones are not compatible, it will not work from you in the earth life to another person in the earth life.

"To work together in earth life, you employ reason to win your argument. Some use force. Compatible vibrations come only when two people team up without trying, as finding themselves in agreement without having a discussion first.

"Team up with us to learn what your tone is, how to make use of this understanding and how to improve your tone to a higher vibration. Knowing your tone will help you understand where you are in the vibratory scale. By becoming the one to use this force field, you will enter into the right group where you can find rest and solace.

"The tone of each person can be adjusted to whatever level and frequency that you want it to be. But only you can make this adjustment. The work we do here is to help you discover just what your vibration level is, you see. Then we can work with you from this point to make any adjustments you wish."

Is it possible, I asked, to find ourselves "at home" with other vibrations, but still be unhappy about being part of this group of people?

"By teaming up with us, you can find your own group. You will either enjoy this level of vibration or you will want better vibrations. Then we will lead you step by step—for that is how we all learn—to give forth the vibrations that will team you up with the group that you (at this point) admire."

Therefore, I concluded, we may be discontented with the group we are in—our friends, acquaintances, close persons—but we cannot move out of that level because of these vibrations that bring us all together. I asked if this conclusion is right.

"Working with us opens your eyes to all the possibilities of life. And you learn that the only way to advance your soul is from the reality to the appearance here on earth. The reality, remember, is your spirit entity, for that is indestructible. So you may understand your own spirit entity better, we will explain this matter of tone.

"Tone is what you have built into your entity by many lifetimes. But this lifetime is one more chance to advance that tone to the goal you have set. Your tone will determine your level of vibration, thus your associations, your teammates, your thoughts to one another. Your vibration determines your level of participation in the work of the godly force or energy. Teaming up with the Brotherhood will enter you to the level where you wish to be."

It seemed to me that what they were saying was that one level was better than another, and I pointed this out to the Brotherhood.

"You will determine this judgment yourself. We do not give judgment upon your soul. Teaming up with us helps you to view yourself against the backdrop of the God of the Universe. That way, you will enter into the good truth that will make you able to see clearly.

"You will understand that the spirit reflects your decisions, and it advances your understanding of the power of the God of the Universe. Tone is what touches the other spirit entities in this universe. Tone enters into the scheme of things as that which is unalterable except by your own will to merge with the truth of God. The *only* way to have the tone that merges with the God of the Universe is to work toward that merger step by step. The one who touches this understanding, but who turns back, or stops altogether, will give his tone no advancement.

"When you do this, you are like the man who went down the right highway to reach the capital city, but when he saw the city in the distance, he stopped to view it awhile. He rested to tell himself how wonderful it was to be so close. Then his vibrations that were so strong came to a halt. He looked back at where he had been, and he regretted leaving so many friends and acquaintances. He told himself that if he went back, he could always make the trip to the capital city some other time.

"Then he went home and soon lost the map that showed him the way to the city. The bright goal faded, and in its place was the humdrum of his life that returned to boredom and distaste for what he did. His old friends teamed up with him again, and he no longer could shake loose of their negative ways. He felt trapped, joined with teammates he did not want. Thus, he gave up his dream, and he sank into the day by day existence that brought no particular happiness or joy. Teaming up with disaster, we call it, because there was the chance, but he turned away.

"The man who turned away is the one who teamed up with his personal ego that refused change, and he turned to earth-mind to give him his truth. He gave up his goal of going into the Promised Land of the oneness with the God of the Universe. He became a turnabout who had a poor tone and therefore, poor vibrations. He chose, you see, not to raise the level of his vibrations.

"But he could have just as well told his friends that he would never see them again because when he got to the capital city, he would never return. But he could not face his people to say the word that ended old relationships and made the past just that—past."

I asked the Brotherhood how tone and its vibrations were any different from the soul growth they have described before.

"The growth of the soul is that which is apparent because you then enact your life according to the growth you have made. But the tone is not apparent because it is that temporary part of you that suggests growth or takes it away. This tone is like being in the water in the bath or swimming, perhaps. The tone is that which surrounds you in the water, the energy that opens the way for the body to move through it. The tone is not visible, but it probes ahead and around us to find new ways to grow. The tone is furthered by your will and your desire. Growth, on the other hand, teams up with your soul and becomes a permanent part of you. Tone can ebb and flow."

It has always seemed to me that people are admired when they keep their old friends. Keeping one's friends is supposed to be the mark of a true character. The Brotherhood responded immediately.

"This is truth for some people, that we should always keep old friends. But perhaps it is not the truth for all persons. It all depends on the inner truth that comes from God-mind. You must get personal truth from God-mind and not depend on others to reveal the truth for you. Absolute truth, remember, is always personal and it always comes from within.

"The tension we speak of in this chapter is taught by us to help you understand how your spirit makes its connection to the mind of God. The tension is that which a person controls just as he might control the tension on the reed of an instrument or on the bow of a violin. The tension you apply to your own person, that inner spirit entity, is that which puts it into a connection with God-mind. To do this correctly, the tension must be understood.

"Tension builds the spirit entity into one whose tone vibrates beautifully. The comparison to an instrument strengthens here. The tone is played, so to speak, to the universe. Tension is applied to your own spirit by teaming up with the Brotherhood or by putting your own spirit into the tension that will make it reach out to the universe to probe for the channel to God-mind. The channel is always there ready to respond to the one who wants this contact. The probe, as it were, works like the antenna of a radio. It senses the vibration you have and puts it into the God-mind wave length.

"This probe enters our own vibrations to become the focus by which the channel is built. The building and probing are all done by the speed of thought. Thought is even faster than the speed of light, believe it or not. Thought is instantaneous, teaming up with what it belongs to. Therefore, when you team up with thoughts that enter willy-nilly without design, you put your own spirit entity into the lower pitch or vibration. The higher vibrations are the ones to aim for, for those vibrations enter into God-mind more easily than lower pitched vibrations."

Wouldn't people find tone, vibration and tension hard to understand in relationship to themselves? Again, I asked the Brotherhood for comment.

"The concept is not as hard as you might think. People understand vibration because they can feel vibration from sound. They know what it is. They understand that radio and television depend on various kinds of vibratory energy to open the sets to receive the programs. Therefore, why is it hard to conceive that our inner selves, unseen to most of you, will have vibrations? No, I think the reader will understand this matter of vibration."

Let me review: Our spirit selves have various tones and vibrations which make us unique. Tone reflects our thoughts, and we can make the tone increase in intensity or decrease in intensity. I asked if this was right.

"This is indeed correct. The increase means that we advance toward our goal of oneness with the God of the Universe. Infrequent vibrations mean, simply, that we leave much space between vibrations for the static of life to creep in, and for interference from other vibrations.

"Entering the truth into your spirit entity helps to close those spaces and increase those vibrations. Team up with us to understand."

Let me continue my review. Our object is to increase the intensity of these vibrations by combining with our personal truth from God-mind. As we increase these vibrations, we live our lives with divine purpose without the interference of other people who might destroy our inspiration or deplete our energy.

"This picture is correct. This means that we have entire charge of our destiny. Isn't it worth the effort to temple with truth? What we present in this book will team up with you and lead you into the best truth for you, the only truth that can help you, personal truth from God-mind.

"The truth that we mentioned in this chapter title forms the basis of all understanding. It is absolute and it is your very own. Teaming up with us will help you to let go of previous terminology that may hold back your spiritual progress, and it will give you the authority to undertake this work we tell you about. Our teamwork will help you to understand all that we say here. Now team up with us to know the truth, the tension and the tone of your own soul."

CHAPTER 11

NEW HOPE REPLACES OLD PLATITUDES

What must I do to be whole?

The spirit/counselor from the Brotherhood began this chapter with no prompting from me.

"People want new hope that God is who He says He Is. They no longer want the old platitudes that many believe are inadequate or untrue. They want what is sure, what belongs to them, what teaches them how to make use of God's power in their lives.

"Teamwork is the answer here. Teamwork will open the way to the power of God in your lives. The truth that enters through God-mind is essential to receiving this power. Therefore, put absolute truth down as the number one ingredient in the teamwork.

"After truth comes the help that you can get from the Brotherhood, that counselor, teacher, communicator that Jesus promised before he left the earth plane. The Brotherhood has the right teacher or counselor for you, and the one who communicates will help you to team up with your helper. The final part of the teamwork is you, of course. Your open being, your open thoughts, your trust in our work comprise the last part of the needed teamwork.

"By means of teamwork you can gather God power into your life. Herein lies the way to produce your good in the life you now live—not some future life, not some future time, not when those immersed in earth truth think you have become perfect. Teamwork is the answer to how to put power in your life, and with power comes new hope for the greatness that God promises to us all.

"When the power of God flows freely in your life, you will hold new hope like a candle to light the darkness. New hope will pour through you and into your lifetime experience as those things you need, that which you desire, that which brings you eternal truth to be used when you need it. The eternal truth, for example, may be used to make your body whole. It may be used to provide your life with prosperity. The eternal truth may now move from the nebulous words that one reads in books into the realm of the practical earth scene. Yes, all this which we now state and much more is possible to you who team up in the way we have described.

"Through the teamwork you will enjoy many benefits. For example, platitudes will no longer hold your attention, for you will understand they come through earth-mind, not God-mind. What is positive, what is useful, what is held out to you through the teamwork may now become a reality in your own life.

"People who want desperately to be one with God tend to stand back from actuality. They never know the God they seek. They speak hopefully, but they do not put themselves into His power, His great energy. This is what *new hope* is all about. This is why we put it into a chapter. New hope could prove to be only a vague hope, not a reality of hope. It is the power of God that makes the difference. It takes people from vagueness to reality. That is our message.

"There are some who have never even explored a relationship with God—not consciously, anyway. But even they enter into the new hope we speak of here. These persons who think they do not need God even now enter into new hope along with the rest of you who consciously want it. People must reach out for God because they are offshoots of God Himself, and therefore, they must seek that inevitable return to the One to whom they belong.

"The team of Brothers along with the one whom you call Jesus the Christ will lead you now into a method or process by which you become one with the truth that will make this new hope your own personal reality.

BECOMING ONE WITH TRUTH
by Jesus

"Unite with us in the temple you have built within you. By now this temple should be a place of great ornate beauty. Here is where we come at your invitation to make this new hope the reality that it must be in your life if it is to be of any worth. Enter your temple, then. Enter it now. Be there in this lovely place you have built and designed. Now invite us through the door you have built for us.

"We come, entering joyously, realizing that you have presented us with a wonderful meeting place where we can work to give you the power that you will demonstrate in your body. Your inner self is your reality, of course, and your body is yours to use for this lifetime. Therefore, we first address the reality of you, your spirit self.

"Team up with us to get this message. Bodily needs that give you anxious moments must not take precedence over our work within your temple. The spiritual work we do is that which will count. It wins its place as most important because it is the spirit that first teams up with power. After the spirit becomes one with power, accepts it and makes it part of itself, then and only then can you put it to work in the outer world.

"Therefore, work at the first, and do not worry about the second at all. There is assurance that if you become one with the power our truth describes to you, then the physical part is easy."

I asked those in the Brotherhood to give us more details to clarify the message further.

"Teaming up with us is simply coming to the temple you have built and then inviting us here. There we are, teamed up to work. Then enter into our counsel in whatever way you

wish. There will be a way we will find together. It is not difficult.

"The difficult part is accepting us at our word. That is where
most falter. Earth-mind enters into people again and again to
counter the truth we bring. We say that this power is now
yours. There it is, accomplished! But earth-mind truth enters
to say, 'Well, that is nice, but you don't feel any different, do
you? I guess it didn't work.' There you are entering the wrong
thought to counteract that which we gave you.

"But there are ways to enter God-mind thought to combine it
with your spirit. First, when we tell you that this power is
yours, believe it with your mind. Then ask God to bless the
thought that has come within you by saying, 'Now, God of the
Universe, power enters my spirit self. Thank you for this great
and wonderful gift. This power is becoming part of me; of this I
am certain. It will not fall away, for it attaches itself to my
spirit. There it is, lifting my spirit into the temple of my being.
There I am floating there with the freedom and joy of the grad-
uated spirit who now has new hope permanently attached. I
am within my temple, the total person who turns to God-mind
for more truth.'

"This power you become one with will never leave your spirit
self because it is now a part of it. Therefore, your spirit self can
now energize your body. Be into this idea. The energy will flow
through your body entering into all parts, energizing itself
into a vehicle that can serve you in playing out your goals,
your good plans. It will literally transform your body as you
submit to the entering and the reentering of it. It will bring
you to higher velocity, higher vibration. Then while the body
vibrates, mold it into that which is perfect. Join with us and
become your own sculptor.

"No disease can survive in a body that is energized by the
power of God. The eternal truth that God pours through the
one with new hope will open every cell to the power of God.
That's the way it is. That's the way we open the door to healing for all people. The only stipulation that is made is that you
must team up with the God of the Universe to accomplish this
healing. The Brotherhood cannot give you what is God's to
give."

I commented to the Brotherhood that Jesus healed others when he was on earth, and he said we can do this healing, too.

"Yes, Jesus opened the door to healing for others. But he did not claim that he did the healing, did he? No! He introduced others to the God Who did the healing. If you want to learn to heal, first let God work through you to heal yourself. Then turn to others with power fully instated within you."

My ring finger has a tingling sensation when I touch my hand in a certain place. Also, a little part of that finger is numb. I asked how I can energize it so it will be whole.

"Your finger must be considered part of the whole. This business of taking a finger or a foot or a toe or an eyelid is not what we speak of here. Wholeness is the perfection that God IS. This perfection is His gift to those who open themselves to the teamwork we spoke of in the beginning of this chapter.

"Perhaps you want to acquire wholeness for your body. This writer wants wholeness, but she tends to focus on the parts of her body rather than the whole. The truth of God is not limited to parts, you must understand.

"There is her temple, big and lovely. Her spirit is there, and we come through the door that she has built just for us. But then she turns herself away from actual oneness with the power that God-mind brings. She will not combine with it unless she lets go of her misunderstandings about her own spirit.

"She enters her temple to become one who does not entirely believe in what she is doing. She comes there as a sightseer, not as a person who lives and belongs there. This temple must be part of her very being. It must reflect her basic spirit. Then she will not view it as a visitor each time she comes. There will be a realization that she is in her own place, the place which is hers, not the place where we put the energy that she may or may not accept. 'Wonderful,' she says. 'This is great,' she notices. But she does not say, 'This is mine.'

"Teaming up with us is step number one. But the second step we cannot do for you or for this writer. This is the one you must do alone. Now claim the power which we give you. It is not to be marveled at as you would marvel at a new and strange thing. It is to be greeted as that which is finally coming to you who deserves it and who wants it. Try it on. How does this power feel? How does it fit? Teaming up with us makes you able to receive all that you will accept in the way of truth. But only you can do the accepting. This part is yours, and yours alone.

"Give your power to your spirit self now. Team up with it in whatever way seems best. This writer has decided to wear it like a raiment! This is all right. It gives her the visualization she needs to make this templing come true. She is getting the idea now. She is assuming the robe of power that entities wear when they become one with that new hope that says God is in the midst of you.

"Work at this. Use your own visualization, whatever it is. This scene in your mind represents that which is happening in actuality within you. Your oneness with power is underway! The teamwork will be that which makes new hope real in your spirit self.

"No one can ever be the most that he wants to be until the power is used properly. Then you can put your body into the condition you want. Here is how it is done.

"Take your body into your thoughts. See it with all its beauty and all its imperfections. Then love your body, and become one with it, and praise it because this is the body that serves you in this lifetime. Now touch it. Take your head between your hands. Then praise God for your head and all its wonderful processes, most of which you do not even understand. Then turn the power toward your head. Visualize this being done. Then turn the God power onto the rest of your body. What happens? Why, your body receives what it needs most—the powerful energy of wholeness.

"The open channel that you form from your mind to God-mind now holds the image of wholeness. The rest is easy! The power has been used to energize your body. You have become open to the process and have accepted it all. Watch the process continue to work, enjoy the greatness performing within you. That which is God has done the work of wholeness.

"Team up with us to understand the truth that we have brought you in this chapter. This truth is easy for us to enter into in this plane of life because here we are spirit. Join with us to make it easy for you, too.

"Now you are growing in spirit, for the God truth of power is one with you. You have moved into a new dimension within the reading of and the working with the words in this chapter. Power opens to your use because you have become part of the teamwork that permits you to open your mind to new hope.

"Tend the truth that is now within you, and never let yourself settle for less than the wholeness which your body can now be. Team up with us to make this truth perform in your life. And never give your attention to any inferior thought, or compromise the thought of wholeness into that which is less. Be one who enters life peacefully, energizing the wonderful truth that you can now believe in with all your heart."

CHAPTER 12

A NEW AGE—A BETTER LIFE

What is this New Age, and how will it affect me?

Every reader of this book knows that life means change. Whether we are ready or not for the changes that occur in our personal lives or in the world we live in, we still must cope with, or better yet, accept change. This chapter deals with change, the kind that will mean the development of a more wholesome earth, and eventually a better kind of life than we know now.

"It is soon time for the New Age to appear," my spirit/ counselor told me. "There will be much change in this earth you live on, but it is not to be feared. This change will clean the air, bring new vegetation and new life all over the planet. The earth will prosper as it did years ago before man polluted it. But man will not know the time nor the exact kind of change that will take place.

"Even scientists today believe there will be some kind of change forthcoming. The teamwork that they share gives them this idea, but they do not feel sure enough of their findings to forecast it. This change will be in the form of the earth center teaming up with a new point in the heavens. This center or core of the earth is tuned into this far point, but it will begin to respond to a different point out there. This will make it enter into a new alignment with the entire universe. That is, the earth will then change to another polarity position.

"As the earth shifts position, people will become very agitated, of course, because the North Pole will be in what has been a warm place. The South Pole, too, will be in a place that people normally think of as warm. The temperatures will alter drastically to reflect the changes, and people will be afraid. But those who understand this change will know that in time things will stabilize.

"This tremendous change in position will mean that some will not continue to live in earth form. But why worry about this? Your souls are eternal! The ones who survive will have a heavy responsibility, of course. But if they understand the truth—and this book will help them be close to the source of all truth—God-mind—then they will receive all necessary help.

"The purpose of this chapter is twofold: first, to give people some idea of the change to come; second, to put them in the frame of mind to accept the New Age as that which is wholesome. Teaming up with us will help you to have this reassurance. Give your inner selves over to the truth of your inner being because this way you can meet any eventuality in life with equanimity.

"Team up with the God of the Universe either directly or through our help. Now put yourself into our counsel. The New Age is that which is good because it is returning the earth to purity. The danger is not from change. Danger lies only in your feelings of not accepting that change."

I doubt if any of us wants this earth of ours to undergo such a change as the Brotherhood outlines. However, they insist that the New Age is something we should welcome because earth-mind truth as we know it today will be wiped out. People will contribute the best of their beliefs to a new and better earth-mind. Reading my less than enthusiastic thoughts on the subject, the Brotherhood responded.

"This view of change is from the perspective of the universe. But you are part of that universe, are you not? Think big here, not small. The earth enters the New Age in order to improve itself. This change will happen as part of the evolution of matter that is God-created. This matter is basically good, and it must return to good. Therefore, the change must happen to return it to the good. You understand this, right?"

Although I indicated that I understood, a change in the earth's polarity position didn't seem like such a great idea to me.

"Now hold the pure thought of this change in your mind. Pure thought has no fear, no worry over change. It merely accepts a change for the better, not for worse. Give yourself over to pure thought here. Think of the earth becoming a better, cleaner, more attractive, purer place that will reflect the God of the Universe.

"Now is the time to contemplate this change, for it will come about in the time that is recorded for it. This time is not given you precisely because it is recorded only where the God of the Universe records such things. But we who rest on advanced planes can see the symptoms that will mean change. These symptoms are clear to us, just as symptoms of disease tell doctors what the disease is. We record these symptoms and know that the earth is now about ready to cleanse itself. Be the one to get ready for this."

Other than accepting this change as good, my next question for the Brotherhood concerned what else we might do to get ready.

"This happening will affect everyone, you know. The thing to prepare for is how to survive without the things you are used to. The books on survival will help you. Survival training in wilderness situations will help, too. But these will not be enough, either. You will need the instruction straight from God-mind on what to do, where to go, how to enter this New Age."

I wondered whether everyone should begin to read survival techniques and to store up supplies.

"Storage is not needed because most buildings will be destroyed as the earth slips and slides into new positions. But knowledge is the main thing here—the kind of knowledge that enters you through your spirit self. That is the reason we bring this up in this book—to assure you that you will not ever be left hopelessly abandoned. You have this resource of God-mind and the Brotherhood who will help you to make the connection.

"To prepare for the time to come, learn how to grow things. Learn how to put seeds into the ground and care for them. Learn about plants. This understanding is important. Then know, too, that you may be living in an entirely different kind of climate than you have before. So you must adapt to change. The mind set here is important, not a knowledge of all climates—the mind set that says the adventure has begun, not the mind set that says terror has started.

"Those who prepare themselves to be a part of this change for the better, and the ones who enter the New Age with optimism, will be the truth in expression. They will be the foundation for generations to come. They will live in peace with all people, and there will be love manifested one to another. People will turn to their inner beings to learn how to become successful in adapting to the New Age. They will team up with us to understand they are not alone. Also they will not grieve for those whose bodies were destroyed, knowing those spirit entities will return to life to populate the earth with good souls again.

"Be into the truth we bring you here; do not let down in despair. Why despair? Have we not told you spirit is the reality? Have we not told you the spirit is that which is indestructible? Give your attention to these words and to the entities who bring it to you. Give yourself over to the understanding that everything that IS comes from the Source, God. This Source, this God, is all good. Therefore, we, the spirit entities, and the substance that makes all creation, must also be good. To prevent the dissipation of good, changes must come about. This is God Principle at work. Now do you understand?

"The entity who writes this has no real concept of this change at all. She has thought about it, and she has considered it in her lifetime. But she cannot fathom this change as actually happening. She has, however, become one with our truth that this happening will occur. Therefore, she wants to protect everyone by telling you where you can go to be safe."

There it was. My spirit/counselor was reading my thoughts again!

"But it would not matter even if we told you such things. You would look about you and decide that you would stay where you are to be with friends, job or whatever. This change will come when it will come. The living of your life until then is what you give your attention to, not to the place on this earth where you want to be so you will be safe. You are safe everywhere, are you not? The spirit is eternal. The body is destructible, yes, but you who lose your body will then team up with your loved ones in the spirit, so why worry over what you call death? Where is the tragedy?"

I suggested that perhaps it was not death I feared, but the possibility of physical suffering.

"Now we have the truth. Suffering in body is what you fear, not death. But if you enter into truth, you will either heal your body or you will learn how to leave it. Then you will still exercise control. Give us your attention on this matter. Learn your lessons well. Take the truth to your souls and you have nothing to fear, NOTHING. Team up with us to help you with this."

Did I understand correctly? Could it be true that we can really heal ourselves or simply elect to leave our bodies if we want to? I asked if this statement is true for us now as well as after the big change in the earth.

"This ability has long been understood on earth and many have done this, you know. To enter the New Age, it might be useful for you to have this understanding safely teamed up within you, right?

"Give your attention to us on the matter of the New Age again. This New Age will bring new leaders to you. The one who now emerges to be the greatest leader is not the ideal one, though he will serve a certain purpose. But he is not the Christ-like person who can lead the earth into an age of peace and prosperity. He is too self-centered, too into his own ego. But he will emerge as a wonderful leader, nevertheless. Give your understanding to this knowledge. The leader who first emerges will not be the one you want permanently in charge. Give him his short tenure, and then get another leader who will be selfless in his approach to the world."

I asked the Brotherhood if I will go into the New Age during my present lifetime. Also, I asked about the readers of this book.

"There will be many of you who will go on to the next plane before this happens, of course. The writer will not be among those who will see the New Age. But her children will see it. They will not accept the truth that this New Age is to come, but they will read her book with interest. It will be that way with many. The children of this writer will be amazed at these words, but because their mother writes them on paper, they will find them hard to accept.

"But in their hearts they will not be surprised when the earth does shift. Only one of them will survive in bodily form to continue into this age, and this person will be helpful to others to give leadership in the time of anxiety. This one will still have this book and will then refer to it and teach others its truth. That is the way this person will stand forth with truth to be helpful."

Predictions about the shift and the coming of a New Age have been made in other writings. At first consideration, it all sounds horrendous. But, as the Brotherhood said, it is a matter of perspective. If we really buy the concept of spirit as our reality, then, as they tell us, we need not be afraid of anything.

The Brotherhood assures us there will be forewarnings of change.

"There will be mentionings of the earth's change in the newspapers. The earth will tremble. The earth will not put out warnings that will frighten, but they will be warnings, nevertheless. These warnings will help you to know that the New Age is entering as you have expected. But you will not panic. The earth will go to a change of good."

I asked for a description of this change as viewed by people living through it.

"There will be differences depending on where you live. The earth will resettle itself and the entire top of it will shift about. The earth will slide, and the entire topography will change. Maps will mean nothing to you, for coastlines will change tremendously. Nothing will be as it was. Houses will fall because they cannot stand the shifting of the earth. The tops of the mountains will fall, and the people will receive new topography everywhere.

"Islands will disappear, coastlines will drop, the ocean bottom will rise, and the entire position of things will change so that you will feel this is indeed a new earth. You will either survive or you will not. But if you survive, there will be no purpose in having supplies, for they will probably be buried in the slide. Therefore, take no thought for such things. What you put inside your mind is what you will have. Therefore, ideas on how to survive are worthwhile at first. Then the agriculture. Then the ideas of how to live together. People will forget about nationalities. They will forget about tribes. They will just be people trying to live and to progress. They will reach out to help others, and they will prosper again."

Could all this be a warning to us to become better people or else this change will occur?

"This change is due to come. It is inevitable. Only the 'when' is not certain. Only God knows this answer, and it is hidden, even from us. We have the perspective, however, to see the coming era and to tell you of it. This message is no trick, for what would be accomplished? A new era will come, and we rejoice in the fact that the earth will be better. Many spirits here return to earth now to take part in the New Age. They enter to be helpful, for they believe they have something to give. These who return team up together to bring earth people into the operation that will prosper them. These spirits have a sense of adventure, and they have a plan before them that they want to enact in their earth lives. They will be strong and will be the ones who can enter this age with enthusiasm."

I wondered if there is anything else, besides what they already mentioned, that we need to know to be prepared for the New Age?

"Preparation is done within the spirit self, of course. The outer world responds to the inner or spirit self. If this spirit self is strong enough in truth, you will survive in body if it is your wish. But if the spirit self is weak with only earth-mind truth, the body will perish because it has no real truth to sustain it.

"Now we will teach you why the earth must have this change. The substance that gives the earth its form, its life and its motion is depleted, and it is not getting nourishment. This depletion is due to the earth-mind truth which draws upon its own substance. For example, earth-mind truth says that this ball of dust and other matter is all there is, and when we believe this, we draw upon the earth substance. However, when we draw upon the substance of the universe, the substance that is unlimited and all good, we replenish the earth substance.

"Therefore, the team that is ahead right now is the team that draws upon the earth's substance. That this could be reversed is always the hope, of course, but the earth's substance at this point is depleted to the point where it must now be stirred up much as a cook stirs the pot to blend good substances. That is what the earth does on its own to replenish itself. People, who are in reality offshoots of the God of the Universe, can replenish this earth, too, by teaming up with the truth that the substance of God brings this replenishment. Then together people literally move mountains to bring about replenishment. But if people turn only to earth-mind truth, there is no replenishment. That is the way of it.

"Now you see why the earth will shift, why people will undergo the change that Jesus forecast. But Jesus did not enter an idea of horror. Entry of the idea of scaring people came later, after Jesus left earth. Jesus wanted only to present the truth to people about their responsibilities, but writers wanted to impress upon mankind their sinful nature and the holocaust.

"Now enter into this truth and consider it. Team up with it. Become one with it. This truth is yours.

"Give your attention now to the entry of the enemy who can destroy all that we work for. This enemy is one who will promise you much to get you to cooperate, but who will team up with no one to do what he says. This enemy has the appearance of good but the nature of evil. This one can destroy entities by pretending to be the Christ returned. But when this entity enters, he will team up only with his own tendencies to perform the teamwork all by himself. He will tell others what to do, but he will not team up with them nor will he team up with us or with the God of the Universe. The truth that you know how to receive will tell you if there is a person who is an enemy, and this understanding will protect you and keep him from gaining power. In this way the enemy is defeated.

"Get your own tone into the tone of the God of the Universe and stay there. If you waver, the truth is weakened, and the enemy can approach. This enemy is the one who leads you from God truth, and who will team up with all that is of earth-mind. He will gain might to be powerful, not to improve the lot of mankind or to improve the earth. Beware of this enemy who will team up with you on the surface level, but who will actually never be one with you or with the God of the Universe."

I asked why this "enemy" is mentioned.

"This enemy will be known to those who survive the era of change. This person will emerge as leader, and many, grateful for leadership, will turn to him with great happiness. But he will lead all astray who give him their time and their energy. This enemy will prosper for awhile, but the people will be in touch with their inner beings—their spirit selves—to know the truth about him. This person who will emerge is the enemy of the age to come, the enemy of peace and brotherly love. He enters only to represent himself, to become a powerful entity on earth. People will give him no power at all, and that way he will fall by the wayside, unhappy, discouraged, rejected. But the world will prosper better without his leadership."

I kept thinking of the enemy as the "Anti-Christ" mentioned in the Bible.

"The Anti-Christ is an idea or a principle that teams up with those who turn their thoughts toward a partnership with earth-mind. Those who want the truth of the earth rather than the truth of God will enter the world to wrest the thoughts of God from those who listen to Him. The principle, however, eternalizes wrong-thinking.

"The leader we speak of is a practitioner of the principle of the Anti-Christ. This enemy, this leader we speak of, teams up with his own ego to enter into the leadership which indicates his power and his strength. He has no use for God-mind truth. He has no use for the truth that is individual. Therefore, he will rely on that which he learned in the former earth-mind, that inferior and useless truth that entered the world before the change. He will team up with what is past rather than what is current. That is why he must be rejected.

"Now pay attention to our promise about our oneness with you and our good counseling. This promise says we will always come when you want us. Believe this and know that you are never alone."

An Addendum to Chapter 12

For the first time, in all of my communications with the Brotherhood, the element of predictions arose. It wasn't so much the prediction that I, the writer, would not live to experience the New Age, nor even the prediction that not all of my children would survive the change in the earth's polarity. As my editor and I re-read the chapter, we were concerned about specific predictions of future events. Would they hurt the overall truth of this chapter? Why were these predictions presented concerning me and my children? What is the point of saying these things? I asked the Brotherhood to comment.

"Team up with us now," the answer began, "to understand how this is not what it may appear. The prediction is that the earth will eventually cleanse itself. The evidence is clear; the optimum truth establishes the necessity for this to occur. The part that you now question is the teamwork involved. The books that we write must survive. To make that happen, we must help the one we think is open to the truth to hold these in trust. The books will enter into the New Age intact because we will help the one who is your child to go to a safe place. Enter our message as openly as possible, not hiding anything.

"The work of our truth must go into the New Age. It will do so because the one we work closely with will heed our understanding and take these books to places where the books will be used to help mankind.

"This person will not be the only one to do this work. There will be others, not your children, who can bring this truth openly into the New Age. Therefore, do not wonder at what we say here. The idea of prediction is interesting, of course, but we do not care to predict just to predict. The truth is the concern here, not the prediction. We enter not into the affairs of mankind to predict this or that happening. We only work with truth."

CHAPTER 13

NEW TRUTH IN OLD WINESKINS

What is new truth, *and·what is the matter with old truth?*

Matthew 9:17—"Neither is new wine put into old wineskins; if it is, the skins burst, and the wine is spilled, and the skins are destroyed; but new wine is put into fresh wineskins, and so both are preserved."

In this chapter the Brotherhood brings fresh insight to Jesus' familiar words quoted above. "Team up with the Brotherhood to enter into a metaphor of the wine and the wineskins. Together we will help you to understand how truth is compared to wine and how your mind is compared to the wineskin. Unite with us to receive insight into the metaphor and into the spiritual work that must be done within you before you can progress past the point of simply receiving truth.

"Team up with us to understand that old wineskins (in the Bible reference) were those people who joined with tradition, the words that were given their fathers. But those who opened their minds and their hearts had new wineskins. They could receive truth that was new to them.

"In this chapter the metaphor has the same meaning. The truth we give must *not* be put into old wineskins, for the old ones will not stand the pressure of the new wine. They cannot bring new truth into expression. That is a fact, you see. We use a wineskin here because those who know the metaphor will understand. Truth-giving is not new, and neither is the old wineskin concept. Those who hold to the old ways will not entirely receive new truth. Only by getting new wineskins—new open minds and new open hearts—will they receive all the truth to be given."

I asked for an interpretation of another reference to wine in Luke 5:39. "And no one after drinking old wine desires new; for he says, 'The old is good.'"

"This part means that people who keep the traditional ways and the truths handed down from generation to generation, will not like new truth. They will believe that the old is good, only the traditional is best. Therefore, they will not receive new truth until the old truth is used up. Those who herald the old ways will not give them up easily. That is what Jesus meant then, and it is the truth today. Those who cling to old truths will not drink the entire truth we give. They may try to mix the two, but then either the wineskins burst with the new energy, or they spill out the new to team up again with the old.

"Get into the spirit of this metaphor. The wineskins that burst will be your own thoughts about your new truth. This may contradict what you have been taught. Therefore, your mind will be in turmoil, saying 'Which shall I believe? Which shall I accept?' That turmoil is the bursting quality we spoke of. Such agitation is not acceptable to most people for long, and they must make a decision. They either combine with new truth and become new persons, or they reject it and go their way with old truth they had stored in their old wineskins—or minds.

"Band together with us to understand how the truth that goes into old wineskins will never help people demonstrate the truth. The genuine truth is, of course, that which comes to you from God-mind. The wineskin is the mind, the indestructible mind that holds your new truth until it is a permanent part of your spirit self.

"Now become one with this understanding: that this mind, this individual mind that we each have, is that which is the spirit's. The brain belongs to the body, and it is matter. The mind, which is spirit, is that which is indestructible, that which is connected to the Mind of the Universe.

"The individual mind teaches us the truth of God-mind, but it is exposed to all kinds of truth. The mind you must give your attention to is that of God-mind.

"Now enter into our best understanding. The good news we bring to you will never enter your spirit self if your mind is filled with old news, old thinking, earth-mind truth or if it is templed with error-thinking that must be abandoned in order to receive new truth. Combining with what is old will spell disaster for the one who has new truth in his mind and wishes to enter it into his spirit.

"Here is the point you must understand—a person has no way to become one with the new truth unless he produces a new wineskin. The new wineskin is the one that has no former thoughts—no stains, as it were. The one that stretches—that is the new wineskin.

"Let us consider how the wineskin helps you to become one with truth. Because it does not have any predisposed ideas, there are no negative thoughts coming from it.

"Old wineskins will never do at all in this new truth we bring you. New truth needs a mind that stretches, a mind that opens itself to enact the truth in this lifetime. The old wineskin, that which the person brought with him or developed in this lifetime, must either be destroyed or thrown out. This is the way of it, the way of becoming one who brings new truth into your being to be enacted in your life."

Over and over again this same idea is expressed, that our minds must stretch to receive and to use God-mind truth. The message is repeated that if we superimpose the new on the old, nothing of value will happen in our lives, for the old ideas, the old philosophies, the old messages will immobilize us. For people who have collected what they think of as a comfortable assortment of truths, this message will not be good news. However, for those who seek that missing link between them and the God that is beyond comprehension, the idea of throwing away old facts, old understandings and the attendant disappointments will be a wholesome concept.

"I still read the Bible, and that is old," I said to my communicator. "What about the Bible? Is it of any value to me?"

"Now be into our teamwork here," came the reply. "The old

is that which was of bygone times. This truth was given for those who lived in the past. The Bible, too, is written for the past. It is a book that records the true spiritual growth of mankind, but it cannot be taken into your present lifetime *as the only guide.* The Bible can teach you many things, but the truth for your soul is not from this Bible anymore than it is from us, this Brotherhood.

"The truth for your own soul is from God-mind. This is what people need and want. This truth must be stored in new wineskins, the open-minded person who does not fight this truth, who does not think of it only as unusual or interesting. Truth will team up with you only if you open your mind toward it, put it in the newness of your soul, not the old self that is teamed up with the old truths. New truth needs the old removed. Then it can work in your life."

Questions clamored for answers. "Why do I find throwing out the old truths frightening? How do I forget those truths I lived by for most of my life? They seem glued to me."

"Team up with us to understand. The new truth that comes to you from God-mind is that which will tear away the old truths. This new truth can eliminate the old and throw it away, letting the new adhere to your very soul. Do not be afraid of anything that comes to you from God. This new truth will come only from Him. Therefore, we know it is good."

There are some who may never believe it right to throw away the old ways, the old beliefs. They may think that the devil himself is part of any plan to throw out old truths.

"Holding to the old ways demonstrates that people are afraid of the new truth. But there is no evil entity. There is no devil. There is only your own team of Brothers who help you here. The evil that mankind fears is not a real entity with power; rather, there is a popular notion that there is a team of the devil and his people who will make you behave in certain ways if you are not strong in God. But the truth is that people use the devil and his so-called force as their escape from personal responsibility.

"The team of God is the truth of the universe. The rest is that which you yourself give power to. If you give power to an evil entity, then there is that evil in your own life. But in reality there is only God. You have created evil in order to give attention to an opposite flow of ideas. This is your escape, not reality at all."

Silently I wondered if it would be better if I never go to church, never read the Bible or listen to ministers? Would it be better not to think of myself as Christian, Jew, Moslem and so forth? Is that how I can have a new wineskin?

As I pondered these questions, the message continued. "There is no way to tell if you should go to church or not go to church. Only God knows your soul. Never think there is one pattern for all. The point of our entire truth is that there is no pattern for you to follow. You are free of all patterns, all previously outlined plans for living your life. Now is the time to discover yourself, to find out who you are in relation to the God of the Universe. God, who is unlimited, does not measure you by church attendance. He does not measure you by the books you read, not even the Bible. But He does want you to open your mind and open your heart to Him that He may give you the truth for your soul.

"God wants you on a personal level, not your earth self, but your God-self. This spirit self of you that wants to unite with Him will learn the how's and the why's of his own life. That is it, simple and straightforward. The writing in this book and in our previous book all adds up to one sentence. God wants to be your partner in the *now* of time and in the wonderful truth He has for you.

"Help us to put your new truth on new shelves within you. Let the old become only a memory, not the truth that you live by. Understand? Therefore, tell the God of the Universe that He is in charge of you, and never think that you will come to evil. There is no God of evil! There is no God who will lead you astray. There is only the ONE God, universal and omnipotent. How could there be a second god who has power when we tell you there is only ONE?

"Those who proclaim a concept of evil do so because they cling to old ways that once were thought creative and good. The old ways used fear to bring people to their knees before

God. But God does not want you to come to Him in fear. He wants you to come in love. Team up with us to enter into a positive relationship and abandon the deceptive one who tells you there is a god of evil. Team up with us to meet a more tender God, a more truthful God, the greatest wonder that we can have in our lives. Turn away from the ridiculous notion that there is a god of evil whom you call the devil or that you erroneously call Satan. God wants no part of such misconceptions. Team up to understand this."

"Let me see if I have this straight," I interrupted. "There is only one God, and He is all good, right? There is no evil spirit that has great power over me or others. The fact of evil in the world is not explained in this way—that there is a devil or Satan who leads people into evil ways."

"You speak the truth," came the reply. "The God of the Universe intends you to be one with Him. The truth inside you wants also to be one with Him. But the power you give to the presence of evil helps to perpetuate it, you see. The evil that men and women do tends to diminish their own spirits, not God's. The evil that people do enters into earth life to affect everyone in some way, but the way to eradicate it is to present this concept of goodness to the world, not the concept of evil. Then we will help people to unite with God who is good, not with a concept of evil that comes from earth-mind truth."

I once had a friend and spiritual advisor who wanted me to become a born again Christian. She laughed about trying to convince me that there is a devil, yet this concept seemed very important to her. "Would you comment?" I asked the Brotherhood.

"This concept of an evil presence within a person indicates a diminishing concept of God," the communicator said firmly. "That anyone would turn to the devil concept after he has known God is incomprehensible to us here. What does make sense is that people enter into a weak God concept, and this concept gives them weak results. Therefore, they turn to some concept of evil to explain why the God concept does not seem to be working in their lives.

"But the nonsensical part of all this is that people who take a weak concept of God receive weakened results on their own through no help from any outside force. If they would instead turn to us and borrow our strong concept of God, then they would demonstrate this wonderful God who powerfully teams up with them. Then people would have no need of this weak entity they call the devil, would they?

"Team up now to understand the wonderful God that we present here. This God is all-powerful, all energy, eternal. He sends the energy of the Universe to you. How can you resist this truth-giving? How can you resist this energy there for you? No past thought or truth you once held dear can compare with this practical yet very beautiful goodness which is God.

"Not everyone will understand this chapter, we fear. There will be many who say to themselves that the Bible says this or it says that. Then there will be the minister who stated this or that also. Their minds will wheel and turn about with confusion, and they will, in the end, reject the new in favor of the old. But this rejection must be accepted by this Brotherhood. Teaming up is not a pure concept for most people. Therefore, they try to compromise. But it is at this point that people either fail or they succeed in making their own God-mind truth work in their lives.

"Take the old metaphor of Jesus into this present time to work the miracles that Jesus knew then and knows now can happen in your life. Team up with us and become new thinkers. Be one who will put a new wineskin into your mind where we will help you get the God-mind truth that will be like new wine. This new truth—this new wine—will begin to team up with the wineskin. The two will work together in harmony to preserve the new wine and make it the perfect expression that it must be if you are to drink it—that is, put it to wonderful use in your life.

"It is time now to go to work within yourself, to become one who will accept the newness of life, as well as the understanding that new truth cannot become what you hope for if it is put into old wineskins or old mindsets. Turn to your inner being who wants to unite with God, who wants to enact your growth plan. Turn to the reality of you and decide at this moment that you will enter all things that God-mind eternalizes, not the things that were brought by other people. Only God-mind should guide you, for it knows you in reality, and it is the Mind which helps us build this wonderful channel that will bring your absolute truth to you. Team up. Team up. Team up."

CHAPTER 14

THE POWER OF GOD—YOURS FOR THE TAKING

How is it possible for me, a human being, to receive the power of God?

Throughout the preceding chapters of this book and also emphasized numerous times in the first book, "The God-Mind Connection," there is one overriding theme or message. Simply put, the message is that unlimited power, unlimited resources are readily available to everyone who teams up with God-mind truth. Therefore, I was very specific in asking the Brotherhood how I, a human being, could receive the power of God.

Their response was most direct. *"The great power of God is yours if you are willing to take it.* Fix your mind on this universal truth we present to you in two parables. In these stories we hide the truth in other objects. The explanation in spiritual terms may be hard for you to understand, but the parables will, we hope, give you the essence of truth that you need to become the truth in action.

"The first parable we present is of two football teams—the team of the God of the Universe and the team called the Requester, one who makes requests of God.

"The Requester wants the God team to play the game without giving their team problems. 'Just win,' the Requester says, 'but don't involve us.' The God team tells the Requester that the team must come out onto the field with Him. This game has rules, and they both must participate. But the Requester says, 'No. You are all powerful. I cannot play in this game or I might get the team hurt. I don't want to do battle here; I just want to capitulate.'

" 'This is really something,' says the God of the Universe. 'So you give up without even coming out onto the field! Now what team would give up without trying?'

" 'The team of the Requester, oh God. We give up to your invincible power. Putting the two of us on the same field to play a game is impossible.'

" 'Teamwork is needed if we are to play the game, Requester! How do we get this game underway if you do not even show up?'

"Now the Requester team is getting the idea. They must come out onto the field to put their teamwork into action. It does not matter if they think they have an inferior team, they must get into the game! The God of the Universe puts His team out on the field and waits. The Requester puts his team out on the field, too.

"According to the rules of the game, the Requester team will always have the advantage, since the God team wants the Requester team to win. The rules are delivered by those who make the game go according to the plan—the Brothers who wear the striped shirts that referees wear.

"The teams begin the game. The Requester team kicks the ball to the God team. The God team catches it and runs toward the Requestor's goal. The Requester team must try to tackle the God who carries the ball. They see Him coming straight down the field, but they think He will swerve this way or that way. Therefore, they do not head directly for Him. They swerve according to the way they think in their minds, and the God team scores a touchdown.

"The point after touchdown gives the Requester problems, too, because they know the God team kicker can kick the ball right through the uprights. They make a halfhearted run to block the ball, and sure enough, the ball goes through the uprights as they had foreseen.

"Now the God team is ahead by a touchdown. The Requester team sees the score and thinks the game is as hopeless as they said in the beginning. They think there is no way to overpower this God team. 'How can we overtake Him?' they ask. 'This God team has a game plan we cannot figure out.'

"The teams line up for the kickoff. This time the God team kicks off to the Requester team. The God team leaves the middle of the field wide open, allowing the Requester runner through. But the Requester runner enters into some fancy footwork to avoid what he thinks must surely be the plan of the God team. Then he trips over his own feet and goes down.

"The Requester team goes into its huddle for the next play. But the quarterback calls such a complicated play that his teammates fall all over each other, fumble and lose the ball to the God team which marches down the field for another score.

"The game goes on in this way with the God team leaving openings for the Requester runners, but they do not take advantage of their opportunities. The Requester team never understands that the God team only wants to make it possible for them to win.

"Need we explain how the game ends? It would appear that the God team wins. But what do they win? The game is not the point, of course. They wanted the Requester team to understand how to win the game and that the God team would help them.

"Team up with the Brotherhood to understand the teamwork involved in this parable of the God team and the Requester team. The God of the Universe comes right at you, the Requester. There you are face to face, so to speak. But the Requester tends to believe that more must be done. Surely he must team up with some church to get God's attention. Or perhaps the Requester must turn himself into a penitent who tries to beg the attention of God.

"Be the one who understands that the God of the Universe is straightforward, not devious. God has no outlandish game plan that keeps you guessing, that keeps you swerving this way and that. He is here, right here, face to face with you. Therefore, team up with Him to know there is no game until the two of you combine forces in a specialized game that will always make you the winner.

"Now team up with us to enter this truth into your being. Team up within your temple, within your beautiful temple that you built to house a child of God. There we come through the door of this temple. We come to enter into this discussion of how to get the power that God has to give you.

"Get yourself into the attitude of wanting this information, of wanting this power in your life. Team up with us to become one who advances toward the God of the Universe instead of going this way or that to play a game of complicated rules. The God of the Universe is here, right here among us. Why turn this way or that in an effort to find Him? Team up with Him where you are, right here in your temple. This will give you the teamwork you need to bring this power straight into your life. There it is, the power of God held in His hands like the football we mentioned in the parable. There He is running right toward you. What do you do? Swerve? Turn this way or that way to show your clever footwork? Where is the ball? There it is not far from you. Reach out your hands. Grab it. Then run the length of the field to your own goal. Team up with us to understand how simple this is. The play is not difficult. The realization of its simplicity is what is difficult.

"Now you have reached the goal, and the score is made. The power is yours. But you return to the field to continue to play because you want this power to enter the teamwork of the God team. There you go down the field again, straight for God. He awaits you with outstretched arms, and you run right into those arms with your power. Then you become one in purpose, one in concept, one in putting the power, which came originally from God, into your being. The game is over then, and both teams won their objective—to make you one with God power. Team up with us, with the Brotherhood to understand this parable and put the meaning to work in your life.

"Now let us work from another angle at this business of getting God power. The teams on the field will not be helpful for all of you, of course, but here is another approach that will give you the same idea.

"The owner/caretaker of a wonderful garden gives it to you so that you may enjoy the many flowers and vegetables. The owner wants you to take care of this beautiful garden, and that way you can have the abundance for your own use. Therefore, you think this is a good deal here. 'The work has already been done for me, and all I must do is take this garden, now grown, and simply see it through its season.' Get into the scene.

"The garden has no weeds nor anything that might hurt its growth. But to keep it in this condition, you must go to work. Now you do not think this gift is quite so great as you thought in the beginning. How can we get this point across? You must work to weed the garden, to put yourself into its midst if you would collect the abundance.

"Great thoughts go through your mind on how to keep the garden going, and you buy magazines on gardening and read them faithfully at night. The next day you intend to work in the garden, but you get out there late. 'There are only a few weeds,' you note. 'There are only a few bugs eating the produce. I think I won't do any more until I read more magazines.' Therefore, you continue to read, but you do not get to work.

"Then you talk to other gardeners. They may tell you they use a wonder spray on their vegetables, but of course it is poison. You consider whether to use the spray or not. You continue to explore all the alternatives. You could write a book on the subject. Finally, the one who gave you the garden returns to see how wonderfully you kept his gift. You are embarrassed, of course, but you explain that it is hard to know what way is right, so you did not do anything.

"The giver of the gift watches you with sad eyes, knowing that you need the produce. He wants to rid you of your indecision, but he cannot do this. He cannot relieve your quandary because the person who wants the produce must act on his own. Tender thoughts go forth to this person to whom the gift is given, but the giver goes away again unable to rectify the problem.

"Do you understand what we mean? The thought of power must be in your mind, in your creative understanding, if it is to come to you. To try to receive it without any act on your part is impossible. You will merely read about it and go your way, and you will say, 'My, this idea of God giving me great power is very interesting, but I must look it up in the Bible and talk to my minister before I decide to try to get it.' The power waits for awhile, but as you talk and as you read, the power concept fades from your inner eyes, and then it is not that which you can collect.

"Tend to your garden if you want its abundance; play the game on the field if you want the power. Take the Brotherhood into your inner being to work with this concept that you may not be left bereft of the power that will make your truth come into full partnership with you. This power thrusts itself into your physical world where you will bring forth whatever it is you need and want. It brings you prosperity, health, and leads you into the fruition of your goals and your ambitions.

"To be a powerful person who demonstrates his own truth, enter into the understanding of this chapter. To be a person who has the truth in manifestation, play the game or tend the garden. There is no standing by in this matter. There is no watering down the truth so that others may accept it. There is only one proven way to demonstrate truth, and that is to take this power and work it into your growth plan. That is the same as playing the game or tending the garden.

"This is our good message to you, that you can be powerful if you choose to be. The power is there for the taking. The God of the Universe does not hide it somewhere or make it difficult for you to get. He offers it to you. Therefore, take it. Be into this message so that you will progress to even higher dimensions of the spirit."

CHAPTER 15

DEMONSTRATING GOD POWER IN OUR LIVES

Intellectually I can accept the power of God in my life, but how can I really make it work?

By now, most of you have noted that this book is written in a progressive sequence. Its purpose is to teach us step by step how to claim the truth of God in order to have successful, joyful, power-filled lives. The chapters are arranged by the Brotherhood to allow each truth to settle into our consciousness before the next logical part is taught. The Brotherhood continues.

"Now you understand how the power of God comes to you, belongs to your spirit and is entirely one with you. This power is yours to command. But how shall you use it in your life? What shall you demonstrate? Here are the questions that need answering, and questions we will address. Naturally the answer is different for different people, but we can provide guidelines to help you.

"The wonderful words we bring to this writer answer her question of how to use the power from God. It is her demonstration of its use, and it illustrates how she can use this power with God's purpose in mind. Teaming up with us, teaming up with God-mind, the news that we help bring comes through her to you.

"Demonstrate this power in your life. It is for the perfection of your soul, not the imperfection. Therefore, the power enters into all projects that increase the perfection of the spirit, and the power decreases when you use it for things that are not part of the God-plan for your growth. We hope you understand this explanation. Your growth plan is for your spirit's perfection in this lifetime, and there are certain things that you want to work out.

"Therefore, *you need to understand your growth plan in order for the power to enhance your life.* This statement is the principle that God puts forth. It is the law. There is no circumventing this law, this principle, so you need to understand this fact up front. The principle is not open to change. It is a law which will stand on the books of the universe until the God of the Universe Himself changes it. Therefore, to make use of this power, you must operate within the right principle. We bring it to your attention so you do not deceive yourself on the ways that this power can be used. Open your mind and your heart to this understanding."

I asked the Brotherhood if what is said regarding the principle, or law, means that our use of God power must be approved by God.

"Not at all! God does not approve or disapprove of your decision. The way to team up with the best use of power is to understand *your own plan.* Your spirit self has a plan that the God of the Universe helped you form before you came to earth life.

"Some spirits enter this life without a plan, but having no plan is disastrous because there is no way to progress from the inner to the outer. These persons wander from one thing to another wondering how their lives should proceed. People must understand their need for a plan, and they can, of course, make this plan now if they wish.

"But if the power is going to work in your life, you must work it into the plan. The two go together—power and plan. That is the way it is, not the way we say it *should* go. The principle applies here, and a principle is that which applies whether or not people beg or they team up with God-mind or any other thing. The power and the plan—they make up the combination that works."

The Brotherhood emphatically underscored the principle, and I tried to apply it to my own life. I asked them about my own plan that calls for me to do this writing, and I asked what else my plan includes.

"The plan that you came with entered when you came into this body only a few short years ago. You had a plan to write the books. And yes, there are other parts of your plan. It calls for you to team up with all the truth possible in this lifetime. Therefore, we work with this goal. The power of God is used by your spirit self to make this happen."

I asked for an example from some other person.

"Many spirit entities who came with growth plans team up with us. One person came to earth to begin the project of helping people demonstrate truth in their lives. He shows others how to do this by helping them understand their growth plans. He enters their spirit selves and reads what is written there. That way he gives the person a record of the plan. But this way is strange to many. Therefore, we want to give you a way to do this on your own.

"Put the team of Brothers there with you in your inner temple. Then enjoy the temple with us. We will team up with you in a gradual way so that you feel comfortable. Then pay attention to those thoughts that you have tried to put aside. There comes the first thought. It is the one that will guide you to your understanding.

"This thought might be of the piano that you bought, that you want to play well. Team up with us to hold this thought for awhile. If the thought burns into your inner being to stay, then pay attention to it. Write it down. Then return to the temple and again meditate. The thought may return. Then write it again and release it. Team up with the Brothers who gather around you. They try to bring forth to your conscious mind what is hidden in your inner mind. A thought begins to emerge. It may seem strange to you. What could it mean? Team up to find out more about it. Then write the thought down, no matter what it is.

"Team up with us to know how a thought emerges. It waits just below the surface of your conscious mind for you to call it forth. Therefore, when you team up within your temple to learn your growth plan, a thought enters your conscious mind. Now enter your temple to see how this works.

"Think about your growth plan, that plan you and God made before you were born. This plan will emerge into conscious reality because you want it. The thought enters your mind, and you must give it attention. Teaming up with us will make the plan more clear to you because we can see it emerge. We understand how it all works—this calling forth of the plan. Team up with us, then, to get it all started."

But what if some people do not have a plan? I asked the Brotherhood about this matter.

"Teaming up with us will make a plan come forth whether or not you made one before your birth. The plan is within your soul—the plan that will improve your spirit self to put it in the realm of the most high God of the Universe. The spirit, and by this we mean all spirits, will team up with the God of the Universe someday. Therefore, the plan must be the bold stroke that lifts the spirit forward. Only your spirit knows what that bold stroke is, and therefore, just any plan cannot be given you. It must emerge from within you. That is the way to get to the point of opening your spirit self to more truth, little by little, in order to grow. Only you know what you will be ready for; only you have the understanding of your own soul.

"The answers are never found by teaming up with outside sources. Only the inner source—the being that is within you—will know what it is that you need to accomplish for this lifetime."

I supposed that we cannot use God power to gather wealth, nor can we use it to benefit ourselves personally in this life. I asked if I was right.

"The first point we make here is that the growth plan must be understood. This step is paramount. But a second point is to understand that God power is yours, and you may use it to enhance your life in whatever way will make the growth plan flourish. This means, doesn't it, that your body needs sustenance, shelter, all the good that will prosper it? How is the spirit to flourish if the body is woebegone? That would not do at all.

"Therefore, the power certainly should be used to put food on the table, to put money in the bank, to bring prosperity of all kinds to you. The spirit self of you will progress among the good things of life probably better than it would among the poor things of life, right? The idea that to flourish spiritually, the body must suffer is the most ridiculous point ever made. The spirit self surely wants the body life to be good. Therefore, let us use power to make the body prosper and be healthy.

"You will understand all things when you know your plan, whatever it is, and you will begin immediately to enact this plan. Then you will be much happier than you have been in the past. Teaming up with the Brotherhood tends to give you the security you need to keep going, to keep on with the plan and to use this power in noble ways. This way you will replenish the power that has a limitless source. To replenish it is to use it in the ways that will make your life the plan. You must see this point, right?"

Once again they read my thoughts.

"This writer thinks that there may be a contradiction here. We say 'noble,' and she thinks right away that prosperity and health are not noble. But they are! The noble act is that which promotes good. If you promote good in your body and in your life, you promote what the God of the Universe expects you to promote. Enter this thought within your inner being, that God will give you more and more power because He wants to see this power used for good. What is the good of power if it goes unclaimed? Power must be claimed, and it must be used. That way there will be enough power and even more for those who reach out for it."

CHAPTER 16

MESSENGERS FROM GOD

How can I develop and use my talents to the highest potential?

All of us want to demonstrate the truth we are learning, for what good is the knowledge of truth without the evidence of it in our lives? In this chapter the Brotherhood presents several messages about the nature of God that can enrich our ability to demonstrate truth.

"The first message comes to you from the one who calls herself the Mother of the New Truth because she has tenderness to put forth. Her message is intended for those who wish more love, more tenderness in their lives. Enter into this truth that God-mind has on the subject of putting more tenderness into your lifetime experience. Team up with the Brotherhood to know that this entity, this Mother of New Truth, is the person she says she is."

FROM THE MOTHER OF NEW TRUTH

"Now put tenderness into yourself by teaming up with Me, the Mother of New Truth. I am that Mother characteristic of the true God of the Universe. Team up with Me, that Mother part of God. Tend My garden that I bestow upon you. Tenderness grows there in the form of the right people who enter your life. Team up with Me, the Mother God who encompasses the nurturing, tender nature which is part of the God of the Universe."

"The team of the Brotherhood knows that every person has specialized needs. No two people want exactly the same thing out of life. Therefore, the Brotherhood addresses the individual here, not the group. Tend to your teamwork that brings you into the game of giving your spirit over to God's purpose. Teamwork is as important as learning personal truth. The two together, teamwork and truth, will make truth demonstrate in whatever way you wish.

"Now give your attention to a message from the spirit who enters here in the name of goodness—the Angel of Mercy. Goodness is Mercy, and Mercy reveals the better nature of mankind."

FROM THE ANGEL OF MERCY

" 'Mercy—what is it?' you ask. I enter the world to give others your best thought, your best gifts of love, of heavenly gifts, of gentleness. I team up with you now on this earth plane to give you gifts.

Here they are; they are yours. To care for them, you must give them to others. The supply is endless if you use the gifts, but if you do not use them, the supply goes away. I, the Angel of Mercy, represent the God of the Universe who has great gifts of goodness for each of you."

"To understand these who come in God's name, join with us to become the heavenly beings who tend to these gifts. Then you will have them forever. They will last beyond physical life, beyond your own tender thought of them. They become heavenly things that adhere to this earth and insert themselves into earth-mind. What greater gifts could you give to earth than this gift to earth-mind?

"Here is the third message of this chapter. This giver of truth enters to give his own greatness to you. This gift is to be used, not to be put into a museum. Greatness teams up to be your own truth in action. It may team up with your least talent to become that which the world awaits. Or, it may team up with your greatest talent to overcome the barriers that man wants to go through, whatever they are. The greatness that enters as your gift comes from one who represents the greatness of the nature of God Himself.

"This entity reveals himself as he who gives you the gift, wants you to take care of the gift, and the one who promises you results if you use it. This entity, this Spirit of the Living God who promises all this, will enter now with the gift. He comes. The greatness is entered into your being, and He smiles at you in benediction. Receive and give of this greatness. Use it and more will come. These gifts proliferate, not diminish. They do this because they enter you in spirit, in the reality of you from the reality of the Universe.

"Now receive another message. The entity who comes now brings as His gift the gift of wholeness. This wholeness represents that which is God perfect, perfect beyond your understanding. This wholeness gives you the positive power of your life, the positive health of your body, the positive power to bring others into this wholeness, too. Become one with him who brings you this gift. This spirit entity who enters now teams up with you in entirety.

"This entity wants to marry you to this understanding. The wholeness that God has to give surmounts any truth that might come to stay with you from earth-mind. The God truth of wholeness beats down any other inferior truth because nothing negative stands against this concept. Put this concept within your spirit, within your spirit entity, within your being who wants this gift to enhance all your lifetime. Take the gift, and then use it in all of your hours.

"This wholeness will not combine with your spirit permanently unless it is used. This gift must be used, tended to by putting it to work. It is like a machine that must be run to stay in good order. If you put it in the garage of your soul, using it only now and then, the wholeness will not work for you because it loses its power. The power, remember, tends to proliferate with use.

"Now enter into our most positive force here, the force of the

God of the Universe, that which everyone wants—the nature of God Himself. This oneness with His nature is the tender gift that now comes to be entirely yours. This oneness with Him is His best gift. But this oneness is contingent upon your receiving all the other gifts. Then when you take them and use them to the fullest, God merges your nature into His, for you show that you become one in your intention, your tenderness, your power, your great understanding.

"This wonderful series of messages teams up with you to bring you into the oneness of our teamwork. We stand here in the place of entry to this second part of life to give this help to you who make the great struggle with your lifetime. This wonderful work here will take you to the heights that spirit can go, and with this ascension there will be a new life on earth, a newness of your truth, your wonderful entity that will make this lifetime the perfect reflection of your spirit.

"Work with us to understand what is given in this chapter. Tend to your gifts. Tend them well by using them wholeheartedly. They will proliferate, never fear. There is no way to use them up.

"Team up with us now to enter into the oneness of God. This oneness is that which takes you to the pure tone of the Godhead. This means that there is one tone, one confident partnership, one tension. Get into this. The oneness concept teams up with the unification that exists when you become the one to use the truth concepts God gives you.

"Extend your thought toward this message we give to you, the reader. The teamwork that you, the Brotherhood and God do together is that which becomes the wondrous work of the Godhead. The Godhead is the trinity of you, this Brotherhood and God. The Godhead that is expressed in the churches is that which combines with the three in one concept of God the Father, God the Son and God the Holy Spirit. This idea got turned around after Jesus' resurrection.

"The Godhead is the three in one—you, the son or daughter; the Brotherhood, who are the entities (including Jesus) who bring the good news through the counseling, the comforting and the Holy Spirit; and God, the one and only God of the Universe.

"Now the truth emerges into the world without any pretense that there is something mysterious that people must enter into. The truth is simple, but people stumble over the simple. We know this, of course. The Holy Spirit, that tender spirit of God Almighty, is ourselves who enter your mind when you invite us to help connect you to God-mind.

"This entire chapter is written to give you messages that will open your eyes even further. Be into our truth here, but turn your mind to the open channel where you will receive personal truth that will enrich your soul. That entire truth you receive will turn your life into the tremendous partnership with God, and you will enter into a powerful period of your lifetime."

CHAPTER 17

TEACHING TRUTH TO OUR CHILDREN

What can we teach our children to help them grow spiritually?

Many times I have thought how much easier it would be for me if I had learned all this truth as a child. How hard it is to unlearn the earth-mind truth I put into my being! Therefore, I am excited about this chapter that teaches us how to bring truth to our children.

"It is important to give your children the concepts that will help them put the God of the Universe into proper perspective in their lives. They must not learn any fearful thought about God, for there is nothing to fear in the true thought about God, you know. The child must not get the idea that God punishes because of wrongdoing. Parents punish, but God does not. God loves. That is the truth. God loves the child no matter what he did or did not do.

"The idea that God holds his love out like a carrot to a rabbit is repulsive. The God of the Universe is only positive, never negative. The child must learn this idea early in life. Never, never teach the thought that God will enter the child's experience as the watcher who disapproves, the watcher who judges, or the watcher who will hurt the child who does something parents disapprove of.

"Why present this weak picture of God to a child? And it is weak, never miss this truth! The entire picture of God is distorted by adults who want to make children behave in ways they want them to behave. This distortion wends its way into the consciousness of children as the truth about God. They cannot see through the deviousness of adults when they are young.

"The confident partnership that each child needs to have with God begins with trust. Trust must be taught, for there is no way to put it across otherwise. Trust enters the child when he sees you trusting God. Then the young one learns it. Team up with us to put trust in the homelife experience so that the child will learn it. This trust is the basis, the foundation for the ongoing relationship with the great God of the Universe. Without that trust, there will probably be a pretty weak concept of God.

"Now pay attention while we outline the needs that every child has. The child first wants to know where you get your strength. In the beginning, he sees you as all-powerful. The child wants to know why you are powerful and how you got that way. That's when you teach the child the answer.

" 'This strength you see in us,' you say to your child, 'comes to us from the great God of the Universe. This God enters us with his power and his strength, and we team up with Him to become the people you see today.'

"The child, in turn, tends to see beyond his parents, beyond them to God. Then he knows all strength and power that comes to the family is brought by this great God. This is the way the child becomes aware that parents are there to help him enter into that same God strength, that God perfection. Words will not teach a child these things in the beginning. Only the entry of truth into the parents will show him who God is.

"Give your child hope that the wonders of this world will be his. Why not? The God of the Universe enters to be the powerful presence that teams up with the child's life, right? Therefore, the greatness that the child begins to put in his mind will come true when he learns to put truth into his being. The parents who teach their children in this manner will cut short the efforts many adults put forth to understand God. These children will team up to use the power of the Godhead—the team of the Brotherhood, the God of the Universe and themselves. That is the trinity. That is the way it works.

"Now hear this thought on teaching children. The child enters the parents' lives to become the joy that they hope for. But they seldom think that this child comes to this life to learn important lessons. Therefore, they can help the child more if they would understand that each child needs to work out his own destiny with the Brotherhood helping. That way the child enters life knowing where to get his help, where to begin his inner search. It is all much easier if the child has the teamwork of this Brotherhood, but the parent needs to teach the child of this.

"Now send your thought toward the child in your own home, the child who wants his life to be wonderful beyond even his own comprehension. This responsibility to make his life all that he hopes begins with your teaching him to hope big. No hope is too big; no hope is too wonderful. Therefore, never put down his hopes. Teach him to visualize them in detail, however. Have him describe them to you, to put them on the shelf of his mind where he can continue to examine them from time to time. They will change and they may tend to fade if they enter into that secret self where God works within him. These hopes and thoughts of the child's life must be encouraged, and if they fade, they fade. God is teaching the child. Do not question. Only accept the outcome. Trust God to help the child. Encourage, but do not take over. That is the way it must be.

"Now enter this thought of how to put new hope into the minds of children who enter into discouragement. The discouragement may come from earth-mind thinking; it may come from those who surround him. Discouragement may team up with his spirit to make him hopeless. But there should not be hopelessness if God is properly understood. That's when you explain that these times of discouragement are only times of change in his life, that change should not be resisted. That's what he is doing—resisting the change, and that brings discouragement.

"The earth-mind destroys hope, and it destroys vision. Therefore, discouragement is a symptom of turning to earth-mind. 'This means you need to get back to God-mind,' you tell the child. 'The way to optimism, the way to success, is through God-mind. The tone will reach out to you,' you tell them, 'and your own tone will happily respond when you team up with the Brotherhood of God.'

"Teach your child that God is that which enters the Universe to make it perfect. Teach him that the God of the Universe teams up with the individual's mind to bring that person the pure and absolute truth about himself. That way the child will learn to listen to the voice within. Much has been written about that voice, but the ear must be trained. The ability to hear that voice does not simply materialize. Team up with the Brotherhood to know how to reach within the child's mind to get him to respond to this voice.

"Team up with us to make the point clear to children that their spirits have been in earth life before. They have lived many lifetimes, and they have learned many lessons that take them to their goal of being one with God. The worth of this concept is to make children take responsibility for their actions. As this concept enters their minds, they reason in this way: 'My inner being is indestructible. Since death has never taken it to destruction, it is eternal. This is great! I am the person in this life that I chose to be. I chose my parents, I chose to enter life with these who surround me. Well, this is where I should be, then. That's why I now accept my team-work with my parents, my friends, my teachers, the wonderful community in which I live. This truth is mine. The knowledge of who I am—that eternal being—is far better than just being John Doe or Mary Smith. Becoming the new person is to my liking. Entering the world many times, surely I will learn many lessons. In fact, I already know many lessons.'

"Give your children the entire truth, not just part of it, for the entire truth will help them enlarge their perspective of this lifetime. Then they will be true to what they understand. They will not heed other ideas that contradict what they have been taught, because the truth will bring them the satisfying life they want. Now put this entire message into your mind that you may bring the truth to your children that will help them learn the pure truth from the God of the Universe."

CHAPTER 18

KNOWING THE GOD OF THE UNIVERSE

What more must I do to live my life successfully?

"To become your potential, you must enlarge your concept of the God of the Universe. It is your concept that determines how well you will express your thoughts into the physical. This means that you want your thoughts—about your goals, expectations, the many needs and wants that you desire—to enter into physical form. Team up with this chapter to learn the basis of how your thought can materialize."

At this point in the book, the reader is ready to collect on that unclaimed truth and put it to work in his or her life. If such a possibility still seems like pie in the sky, put the book down now, for nothing more can be said to make this truth practical. However, if you are even now visualizing a life full of new energy, new talents, new successes, then read on.

"To express your thoughts into things, to understand your potential, you must enter the team of the Brotherhood, God and you. That you may understand fully, we present this chapter on building an enlarged concept of God. First, you must embrace the individual truth that the God of the Universe has to teach. Second, you must enlarge your concept of God beyond the meager one with which you entered life.

"Team up with us to put your mind into God-mind. In this way you will learn of this wonderful God, the One who teams up with us and who teams up with you to bring you this truth. Now open your heart and open your mind to this truth, to this open channel to God-mind.

"Join us to know the greatness that God has within Himself to present to you, the child of His truth. This greatness opens your mind to becoming one with truth. The God of the Universe enters into no one without bringing the whole God concept. The person may elect to use only part of that greatness for one reason or another, but nevertheless, God comes with the entire package of greatness.

"No person enters into the entire picture of God without the assimilation of the truth from God-mind which teaches the soul the greatness of God. Team up to understand that *greatness* is the totality of what we call God. No word will encompass his being like this one word. No word will come as close to describing what God is than this word 'great.' That is why we spend time on this.

"Now open your mind to this greatness we speak of. Open your mind to the greatness which is God. This team of you, the Brotherhood and God (the trinity) will open the way for you to perceive that greatness you need to put your life into its fullest potential.

"The God of the Universe waits to team up with you. He does not beg you. He does not wait outside your door at night to grab you when you least suspect and to punish you for not seeking Him. He is not capable of evil intention nor the tendencies that mankind give to Him of being the One who judges your soul. The Bible stresses judgment because people entered this belief into it. God did not enter it. God entered His entire greatness. That is why we must open your eyes to this concept of the greatness of God to get you away from the lowly tendencies of putting God into man-made truth forms.

"No one who wants to enlarge the concept of God can hold to the old concepts. Those must be abandoned to allow your mind to expand. The parable of new wine in new wineskins applies here. The truth we get to you through God-mind tells you now that those who want this enlarged concept must combine with a new concept. God is NOT the *person* who enters into the ravages of emotion and hate. God is NOT the entity who enters into the idea of 'you love Him and He loves you.' This God is great, not lowly. This God is completely entered into the power of good and the power of truth. He uses his teamwork to bring you, His entities, into His Being to be one with Him, to be the ones to understand complete freedom.

"This entity that you are will not advance to this wonderful concept without work on your part and teamwork on the part of the Brotherhood. Then the God of the Universe enters into you and you into Him to become one, and the goal is met. Unite with us to know the God of the Universe, the God who enters into this writing to present His truth to you, the reader.

"Now pay attention to the next part of this chapter. It will combine with your good wealth of truth to move you forward. You will then allow your concept of God to advance to a higher vibration, which is our intent, of course. This advancement may be done again and again as you progress, and that is how you will enter the truth that God is much more than you ever supposed or hoped for.

"Now bring your entire entity into our good presence within your temple. The truth that you have put within your temple awaits you. Place your confidence in this truth. Now, will you become one with this truth? If the answer is yes, enter into your new team of the Brotherhood, God and you. Together we put this truth onto your soul with indelible ink. There will be no way to erase it from now on. This truth is one with you. Team up to make this happen.

"The truth you want to put into your spirit self will become one with you if you tell it to do this. 'Be the truth that extends my concept of the God of the Universe,' you say to it. 'Team up with me in this temple.' Tell the body to rest while this templing takes place. 'Take this time to become quiet,' you say to your body. Tell it to become the tender truth in expression by helping you put new truth into your soul. The body will cooperate because you rule the body, not the other way around. Team up to make this truth of the concept of God your very own."

"Even if we can only extend our concept a little bit," I asked, "can we consider this progress? We might *want* the entire concept, but if we fail to get it all, do we enter what we can get?"

"Try to understand that entities the world over want this concept within them. You put your foot in the door, so to speak. Then keep working until you get your entire self inside. This means that even a little bit is worthwhile. The whole concept is worth accepting, even if it's only bit by bit.

"Now write your understanding of the God concept down on paper. Then hold that concept in your mind, and study it to know how far you have come and how far you have to go. If there is any reservation about God, there is more truth to be absorbed. The truth you already have is not to be given disrespect, however. This truth is worthwhile. Therefore, praise it for the truth it is. Just recognize that you must go even farther."

I wondered if we must use individual truth from God-mind rather than universal truth to get to the highest possible concept of God.

"This is the teaching—that the God concept we all want in our hearts and in our minds comes to us bit by bit as we are able to absorb it. Therefore, though we could teach this concept as to a class, the entire class would not progress together. The class members learn at individual rates due to their differences, right? That is the way it is with truth.

"The reason we say that the best God concept is greatness is that it encompasses all that we have taught you bit by bit throughout the book. But now it is time to review, to test yourself, to become the one to evaluate your own progress. Remember, God does not evaluate you. He only wants to give you these great gifts that we have spoken of in other chapters.

"We speak now of greatness to open your eyes to your own truth that you have bound to your spirit. If the truth is insufficient, there will be no greatness concept. There will still be fear concepts and other negative concepts of God that cause you to shy away from the idea that God is indeed great. This is the supreme test you must pass. Team up with us to extend your concept until you say without qualifications that God is indeed great.

"To become the person who teams up with your own potential, you must team up with the entire truth of God. To admit this God-mind truth to your inner being, you must get all false concepts out of the way. To enter into negative concepts is to enter into false truth. Only the person who enters into positive truth will be able to produce his potential.

"Now pay attention to the rest of this chapter. Team up with the God of the Universe who wants to awaken you to the tremendous personage that He is. With this concept of the Great God of the Universe instilled within you, you may become that great personage. That is the way the entity who wants this advanced God concept can regard himself because the God of the Universe shares the thoughts that teach you how to use greatness. That way you will become all that you dream of and more. Those goals you wrote in the beginning will take on deeper and deeper meaning, and they will undergo change that you never dreamed possible when this book began. Those goals you wrote then—have they not undergone much change? They will reflect the God concept you have to a greater and greater extent because your own concept grows and grows.

"Be into our good truth and do not turn away sorrowfully because it is too hard to do. The rich man whom Jesus admonished to team up with the truth of God and sell the possessions he had represents you who refuse to tear out the old truth. The rest of you who have torn it away in favor of the new plan will team up with the greatness concept of the God of the Universe. Then God will team up with you to put you into this same concept beside Him.

"Now enter into this teamwork, into this trinity that puts the truth into your own being and into the demonstration that reveals the great God of the Universe. Give your whole attention to this entity who inhabits your body for this lifetime. This entity wants to team up with this trinity to become the one to understand the greatness concept. That is the purpose of this chapter.

"Now become still. Enter quietly into our presence within your temple. The God of the Universe enters here also, but we do not picture God entering. We *experience* God entering. His enduring truth teams up with us to bring us into the Perfection that He is, into the Joy that He is. Team up with us to make this come about in your life. Enter. Give your thoughts to what is happening, and the thought that God is what He says He is manifests within you. The greatness concept is yours forever.

"Send your thought now to your outer expressions—to your body, to your surroundings on the earth. These change to become that which the God of the Universe enters, not what you enter. Therefore, they become more beautiful, more intense, more tender and more pure. Team up to know this truth entering into your being and manifesting to the physical. These two acts—the thought you present to the God of your being, and the teaming up with God-mind truth—these will join together in manifesting your goals, your ambitions, hopes and dreams into outer expression.

"Now place your own being in our care to receive our wondrous perfection that we combine to give you. Our help is always here. Send your best thought toward us, and we respond. The fellowship is that which will give you the gentle touch of the bright sun of God.

"Now the chapter is complete."

CHAPTER 19

TENDERNESS TO YOU, THE READER

How can I fulfill the deep longing of my soul for tenderness?

Again and again in this book comes the message that truth becomes part of our inner selves little by little. Impatient by nature, I decided that a slow progression such as the Brotherhood described was not for me. I would read this truth, think on it and simply accept it. Surely I could make God-mind truth my own truth very quickly.

Intellectually I accepted the new truth, but my life did not change as much as I had hoped it would. Demonstration of my thoughts into things still seemed a far away hope rather than a reality. And though I had earlier manifested good health, I began to have symptoms of certain physical problems that I thought I had overcome.

In private counseling, the Brotherhood urged me to spend more time in my inner temple to combine with the truth I had stored there. Some days I would follow this suggestion. Other days I felt pretty good about myself and would not even approach my inner temple except to work on the book.

One day I expressed a personal need to the Brotherhood, and here is the response.

"We will tend to this need in the bosom of your temple where we talk to you. Go to your temple often. Then you will not become depressed or unhappy as you are today. Temple with the truth, and go into your inner temple frequently. That is the way to overcome a life that teams up with earth-mind truth."

Another day I expressed my agitation over a certain person who stirred up much unhappiness with a family member.

"Be the one *not* to hate, *not* to seek revenge, *not* to want hostility to continue. Tender your thought in happy ways, toward intended good, toward the Being of Tenderness who has the right gift that you need now. Team up with us, not earth-mind thoughts."

This Being of Tenderness, one aspect of God, is a truth I must make part of my own being so that I can do what the advice and counsel suggest. How can I demonstrate tenderness, for example, if I don't accept the tender nature of God? How can I demonstrate any truth that is not part of my own soul? This chapter about tenderness challenges, yet encourages us, in our quest of oneness with God.

"The team of you, the Brotherhood and God enter into teamwork to teach the truth of the tender mercies to your soul. The team wants to teach this so you can demonstrate tender mercies that you need in your life—those that you need to extend to other people, and those that others will extend to you. Becoming part of this teamwork will enable you to demonstrate this wonderful quality of life.

"The God of the Universe opens your eyes to His entire truth. Team up with us to move forward to a demonstration that is not only possible, but which proves your new truth. In this way you see tenderness demonstrated in this lifetime. That is what the chapter is about. Team up with us to realize this truth.

"Now put your inner self into our good hands. We meet you in your temple where we do our work together. Team up with us—that is, put your mind into a neutral position to receive. Team up with us to know our presence is the reality in your temple, not a hopeful nothing. Now put your greatness concept into this temple. Extend your concept of God as far as you can, ever mindful that the goal is greatness. In this way you enter the new truth of this chapter.

"Here is the truth. He who would put mercy and tenderness

into his life must open his mind and his heart to this Brotherhood and to the God-mind. Then he will receive those gentle attributes in his life that he most longs for.

"Everyone wants love, right? Everyone wants others to believe in him, right? Team up with us to have these qualities in your life. Team up with us to demonstrate tenderness. Without tenderness, you would not prosper and become the person you want to be. You would be a shell without substance. The shell is the prosperous person who teams up with the good of his life. The whole person teams up with tenderness because it is equally as important. This new truth will enter into your being to enlarge your concept of God. Tenderness is that eternal truth of God that many people need but that many people think impossible to demonstrate in this lifetime."

"Why", I asked, "do so many people think tenderness is impossible to demonstrate in this lifetime?"

"We team up to bring you the truth, but you team up with earth-mind that tells you that you should expect nothing in this lifetime in the way of tenderness. The earth-mind tells you that the tender mercies are few and far between. The earth-mind truth tells you that good friends tend to desert you, to abandon you when the going gets tough. You are lucky, earth-mind says, if you have only one good friend in this lifetime. The earth-mind tells you this and it tells you that, and you team up with all those thoughts. Then the God-mind truth is ineffective. That is why people think tenderness is impossible.

"Now put your new truth to work. This is the way it must combine with you. First, enter it into your mind and into the tone that continually reaches out for truth. Second, give your thought to your inner being that you want to become one with this truth, that you want this truth to belong to you. Finally, team up with us to put this tenderness into your own being. When your truth is one with you, you can attract the tenderness you need in the outer reaches of your life. Team up with this truth."

I asked for an explanation about how the truth concerning tenderness can change a person's life?

"Perfect understanding of tenderness will end your tendencies to like only those people who enter your very close range of vibration. This way you can extend tenderness even to those outside your vibration field. To become a person who reaches beyond your own vibration field, you must enter the tenderness truth into your being. Then, when this is entered, you will not only be able to reach out to others in different vibration levels, but you will attract their tenderness toward you.

"Teaming up with this truth will make your life far more pleasant than if you do not enter it into your being. Without tenderness, you may have abrasive problems with other people. Teaming up with tenderness, however, will make your teamwork with others tender, understanding, thoughtful. This way you will have the greatness of God Himself.

"The tenderness that enters your inner self brings great beings into your life. By this we mean that others who have tenderness will enter your life. Tenderness will surround you and abound in the activity of your life. Be the one to collect this benefit that the great God of the Universe has to give you. Put the other benefits of God into perspective, and you see that tenderness puts your life into a frame that the rest of the picture needs. Tenderness frames your life and holds the other gifts in perspective where you can view them properly. But do not neglect this frame, for the picture is incomplete without it.

"Need we point out to you how much your life will change and improve with this beautiful picture hung in your inner temple? Hang it there now—the frame that is tenderness, and the picture which contains all the gifts that you want from God. This picture is not static. This picture vibrates with pulsating energy that gets the eye to focus on the center of the energy which is God Himself. The picture will disappear if there is no understanding of its source—God. The picture will temple with your spirit if God is the center of your understanding.

"Give your gentle touch of tenderness to the one who writes this book. Tenderness is entering her temple now as the frame that is beautiful with the burnished eternal glow of God light. The temple reflects this glow. Now the other gifts enter to be part of the picture which teams up with her soul to become that which pulsates with God life and which teaches her to reach forth to take God's gifts. Teaming up is what she does best. That is why the picture enters her temple to become her own.

"Now it is your turn, dear reader. Team up with the tenderness that God gives without ration. Take the tenderness that God IS and put it into your own temple in the form of the frame that holds together all the other good gifts of God. Take this frame into your mind to create it however you wish. The spirit self of you will rework the frame until it is your frame and yours only. Give your attention to us in this matter. Give your attention to our partnership with this new truth that will now become the gentle touch of God that enhances your lifetime experience."

CHAPTER 20

THE NEW TEAM—THE READER, THE BROTHERHOOD AND GOD

How can I claim my truth and put it into material form?

If you have read this book up to this point, no doubt you are already part of this special team that the Brotherhood refers to as the trinity. You, with the Brotherhood and God, are now one unit, one team united in the hope of making the truth of God-mind one with your soul.

"Now is the time for this teamwork that advances your own growth," the Brotherhood states. "Therefore, turn yourself toward this teamwork, and we will work to make your own lifetime experience that which will advance your soul."

They remind us that Jesus, the Brother of Brothers, pointed the way toward the Counselor, Comforter and Spirit guide.

"This is the great promise Jesus made to those whom he left behind when he ascended into heaven, that you would not be left without comfort, without help, without guidance. Send your thought to this entity, Jesus, that you want to understand the Brotherhood, and he will make it clear to you. The Jesus you know will then explain how the Brotherhood works. He will come directly to you, and you and you.

"This team, that empties you of earth-mind truth and inserts God-mind truth in its place, brings you the hope of turning God's promises into reality. This is the way it works. As you insert truth into your being, hope turns into reality. Give us your open mind, your open heart, your spirit that unfolds itself to enter new truth. This way you will grow spiritually into the tender bloom of God-like spirit. Then you will team up with your body to demonstrate the truth in the outer expressions of life. This is the promise, and this will be true in your life if you want it.

"Need we explain this detail by detail, or do you now think you understand?" Again they read my thoughts which persisted in requesting more explanation. "Teaming up with the Brotherhood and God-mind enhances the lifetime experience to one of ecstasy, of wonder, of extraordinary experience. This teamwork will advance you to the point of being able to connect to God-mind on your own without the help of the Brotherhood. This advancement will then take you to the other planes of life, beyond this plane, far beyond this second level. That is how much you can advance your spirit self.

"Need we tell you what this means to you, to the inner being of you?" Perhaps I should have known the answer, but a response came anyway. "To advance beyond this second level means you will not return to earth life again unless you return for the purpose of bringing special information or special help. Teamwork that we do together teaches you far faster than living lifetime after lifetime. This way you learn and apply what you learn at the same time. This is how you can go so fast in your advancement.

"Now put yourself into your temple. This temple by now should have been altered over and over. It will undergo even more altering to make it what you need as you enter more and more truth during your lifetime. Your temple teaches you many things. It teaches you how to use your mind to visualize things in detail. Your temple also teaches you to put things into your mind that unite with your inner being. Team up with this temple to understand how it teaches you and how you can make use of it. The temple is your center of worship, not your church, for the temple houses the reality of you, your spirit self, that enters there to become one with truth. Be the one to know how your temple works to help you demonstrate truth.

"Never tell the mind that there is no need of the temple, for that would be undermining the entire project. The temple is essential to your progress here in this lifetime experience. To do away with it is to depend on earth-mind truth, and you know that is disastrous.

"Open your mind to the newest understanding that we leave with you. The truth center (temple) that you build within your mind unites with your new truth. This truth center teaches you the gentle goodness of God, the pure truth of God-mind, the open heart and the open mind that get their truth from the true source. The truth center is that temple within you, that place where you worship, that place where you meditate, that place where God deals with you in His mercy, His understanding, His pure and tender love.

"Now enter your temple to put your own spirit self in order. Team up with us daily to do this thing. Put your life in order. The person who writes this book puts her own self into order before she writes, or else she cannot write. Her life gives her problems to work out, questions which she wants answers for, heartaches that need resolving, and thoughts of earth-mind that intrude themselves onto her spirit to wet down the good truth from God-mind. Then she goes to her temple to talk with us, to listen to God-mind, to emerge victorious over her doubts, her fears, her teeming earth-mind thoughts.

"When you have put the temple of your soul in order, take the picture we described to you earlier and hang it in a good spot where you view it each day. Is the frame well dusted, beautifully finished, glowing? The objects in the picture—are they what you wish to manifest in your life? These things enter the picture, change, enter again, change into something better, and so forth. This picture is never static, for the energy flows and flows. That's the way it works for you.

"Now team up with us to enter the truth of this book into your soul. Take each chapter and review. Have you taken the truth into your spirit self? Have you written down your goals, adjusted them as God-mind teamed up with you to give you greater understanding about yourself? Have you centered your mind in teaming up with God-mind? Get the Brotherhood's help to form the channel to God-mind until you can do this on your own. Then team up with the trinity as we outlined it to you. Teaming up in this way holds you fast to God-mind truth and empties the earth-mind truth that wants to enter and hide away inside your being where the light does not reach.

"Turn yourself inside out, and let the light of God shine on every part of your soul, nothing withheld. Then the earth-mind truth will vanish, and in its place is the God-mind truth all by itself. That way you will turn yourself into the spirit that unites with the God of the Universe. That way you will be the person you always wanted to be in your heart of hearts.

"Now this book is completed. Though this book ends, your advancement does not end. Team up to make the most of this lifetime experience. Team up to enter the truth, to enter into counsel, to become the most that you can be. This is our team-work here that reaches out to you to make your dreams and your hopes and your goals manifest into the perfect demon-stration."

Books and Products to help establish
The Global Spiritual Awakening

Jean Foster is an important new writer, a very clear channel and one of the many now appearing to show the way to the New Age. Her first book, "The God-Mind Connection," was published in early 1987 and has already touched the lives of many. The final book of her first trilogy will be available in early 1988. A second trilogy is then planned.

In the meantime, we at Uni ∗ Sun will do our best to publish books and offer products that make a real contribution to the global spiritual awakening that has already begun on this planet. For a free copy of our catalogue, please write to:

Uni ∗ Sun
P. O. Box 25421
Kansas City, Missouri 64119
U.S.A.